The Worst Team Ever
An Inspiring Soccer Chapter Book for Kids about Growth Mindset

Written by Mateo Sommer

Illustrations by Henrique C. Rampazzo

Production management by Magdalene Ward

This book is a work of fiction. Characters and events in this novel are the product of the author's imagination. Any similarity to persons living or dead is purely coincidental.

For information address LittleBigPage, 312 W. 2nd St #1934
Casper, WY 82601, United States.

Paperback ISBN: 9788367973199

First Edition

The WORST TEAM EVER

MATEO SOMMER

 You can **download the free audiobook** version of this book.
Go to the *last page* for more information!

Contents

Ms. Voss

Gabriel

Benji

Daniel

Grandpa Hugo

Oliver

Rosie

Noah

chapter #1
New Beginnings

NOAH STOOD back from the bathroom mirror and looked at his appearance. As he brushed his hair down to cover his cochlear implant, he decided with a sigh that he would do. It was the first day of school, but with a difference. The school was brand new and had been built so that children living in his area no longer had to travel miles every day. His old school had been far away, and he was happy this new one was so much closer to home. He also knew that all the local kids—just like him—would be going there.

"Noah! Come on, son, get some breakfast. We have to go in twenty minutes!" Mom usually worked from home, but she had to go into the office once or twice a week. Today was one of those days, which wasn't helping Noah's nerves. Mom was usually good at spotting his anxiety and calming him down, but today she was fussing about her meeting.

"Coming!" he called, turning his back on his reflection and picking up his backpack from the bedroom doorway. "Is Dad still here?" he asked hopefully as he entered the kitchen and put some bread in the toaster.

"Oh, no, honey. Dad had to go in early today—a big break in a case, apparently. He wished you good luck for today, though."

Noah choked down his toast while he waited for Mom to double-check that she had everything. The breakfast seemed to stick in his throat as he thought of all the new kids he would meet at school. He wished for the day to be over already.

Mom seemed to pick up on his thoughts. "Come on, chin up, Noah," she said kindly. "Maybe you'll make a good friend today. That'll make everything better, won't it?"

Noah thought about it, then nodded. "It would. That would be really nice!"

"Well, then, that's what we'll hope for," Mom said briskly. "I'm ready, let's go!"

Waving goodbye to Mom a few minutes later, Noah forced a confident smile onto his face. Mom looked worried about her meeting. She seemed to feel guilty that it was also Noah's first day at the new school. He wanted her to think that he was just fine, so she could focus on her presentation for work. He watched her drive away, her hand fluttering a goodbye as she pulled out of the school grounds, then turned to find his new classroom. There were class lists lining the walls of the reception area, and Noah found his name fairly easily. But as he ran his finger down the lists of names, he heard all the children crowding around him. They were calling out to each other, and a lot of them already seemed to be friends. Noah felt lost—alone among a huge, chattering crowd of people. He felt tears prickle in his eyes and his throat clenched up.

No! He wouldn't cry here and now. If he did, he would never live down the shame of it. For a brief moment, he imagined being an adult. He saw himself in the future, overhearing whispers as he did the grocery shopping, whispers that he had been the boy who'd cried on his first day at the new school a long time ago. Noah swallowed hard and focused on his classroom number, and the awful, close-to-tears moment finally passed.

As he moved toward his new homeroom, he heard another boy behind him talking to others who were headed in the same direction.

"Hi! I'm Daniel. I'm the cool kid, so if you're friends with me, you're cool too!"

"Oh, right." One of the other boys laughed. "Guess we'd better be friends with you then."

"That's right." Daniel grinned, coming into view. His big smile made the other boys smile back. The small group, now all laughing and talking happily, introduced themselves to Daniel. As they did, they moved past Noah, and all headed in the same direction.

Noah followed at a slower pace, his mind full of admiration for Daniel's easy confidence. He thought, *I wonder what would happen if I did that?* He imagined the other children turning their backs on him, sneers of disdain shooting in his direction, their smiles sliding off their faces.

He sighed heavily and trudged along, wishing with all his heart that he wasn't so nervous and awkward around other people.

For his part, unlike Noah, Daniel wasn't nervous at all. For him, it was almost normal to be going to a new school at the beginning of each semester. He had perfected the art of sliding into a group of friendly-looking kids to get to know them quickly. As he made his way

to homeroom with the others, Daniel noticed the tall, pale boy they had overtaken. He had . . . *something* . . . in his hair? Wondering what it was, while maintaining his bright smile and casual attitude, Daniel thought, *he doesn't need attention, not like I do. I wish I could be like that.*

"Hey, Daniel?" One of the boys he had joined turned back to him.

Daniel tore his attention away from Noah. "Yeah, what's up?"

The boy gestured around them. "Do you . . . like . . . know lots of people here?"

"Ha! No way!" Daniel replied. "I'm just really good at starting new schools. My parents move a lot, so I've had a lot of practice."

They stared at him, and Daniel was aware of the pale boy hanging out at the edge of their group. He seemed to be going to the same class.

Daniel explained, "My mom's a travel writer, and my dad's a business consultant, so they both need to get around a lot, all over the place. Every six months or so they find a new place for Mom to write about and research and for Dad to line up new business contacts.

We pack up everything and move. I've lived in just about every place you can imagine."

"Whoa," said one of the boys. "That must be so cool!"

Daniel smiled, but Noah thought he could detect a note of brittleness in there too.

"Yeah," said Daniel. "It is very cool. But," he added, and now there was a note of desire in there, "I would like to spend a bit longer in one place. You know . . ." He caught himself and forced a laugh into his voice. "Be able to know which teachers are the ones who let you mess around in class."

The boys laughed and they all trooped into the nearly full classroom. Looking slightly frazzled, the teacher was standing behind her desk, a list of names in her hand.

The first hours of school flew by, as the teacher took roll, explained about recess and lunchtime, and they played icebreaker games to get to know each other. Finally, the teacher said it was time to get changed for gym class. They were supposed to bring athletic clothes from home that day, and they had, which earned them a beaming smile from the teacher.

Noah changed quickly, and as always, stood with his cochlear implant on the side closest to the wall.

He wasn't ashamed of being hard of hearing, but he hated it when people asked him questions. It was hard to know what to say to "What's it like being deaf?" when you'd never been anything else.

In the gym, there were soccer balls stacked to one side. Daniel was still in the center of a group of boys, but he broke away to grab a ball for himself. He proceeded to show off a bit by juggling it around his whole body, bouncing the ball from his head to one foot and back again, then rolling the ball up one arm, over his shoulders, and down the other. The students crowded around, alternately teasing and cheering him on. Noah watched, a little sourly. The feeling only deepened when the gym class teacher came in and saw Daniel messing around.

"That's very good, young man," she said. "What's your name?"

"Daniel, ma'am," he replied politely.

"Great, I'm Ms. Voss," she said. "I run a soccer club after school. It was a private social club, but we're bringing it into the school now. Why don't you come along and try out for the team? We could use some good players to add to the mix."

A group of boys standing off to the side muttered something and then laughed meanly. Noah wondered what they were laughing at. He would have *loved* to be invited to join the club.

"I'd like to!" Daniel exclaimed. "I'm gonna be a famous soccer player when I'm older. Just you wait and see!"

One of the group of boys laughed so hard this time that he doubled over, his face red and he was gasping for air. Ms. Voss ignored them, but Noah saw her face pinken slightly. He decided to be brave for a change and headed over to her.

There was a girl already there, asking her own questions. "Is there a girls' soccer team?"

"I'm sorry, Rosie," Ms. Voss said. "I've been campaigning for one for years, but no one really seems interested in helping us get off the ground."

Rosie's expression fell.

"But," Ms. Voss added gently, "now that the school is open, maybe we can get more girls interested in playing."

Rosie nodded, but she still looked sad.

"Keep coming to the club, though," Ms. Voss encouraged. "You're easily the best player I have."

Rosie smiled a little at the praise and nodded. She returned to the other girls who were standing in a huddle on one side of the room. Noah moved a little closer.

"Um . . . Ms. Voss?" he started shyly.

"Yes?" She turned to him, and he noticed her swift glance at his cochlear implant. "It's Noah, right?"

"Yes, ma'am. Um . . . I'd like to join the soccer team too." Noah hesitated, seeing a blank expression spread over her face. "I've been practicing really hard over the summer. Could I at least try out?"

Her face cleared into a warm smile. "Of course you can! Come and get a sign-up form at the end of class. Your parents will need to sign it. And let me know if you have any, uh, special requirements." She touched the side of her head as she spoke, and Noah realized she meant his implant.

"Oh." He smiled a little, raising his own hand to the implant. "No, it's fine. As long as it doesn't get whacked with the ball or anything."

"OK, that's good to know." Ms. Voss returned his smile. "Then, just their permission to sign up is required."

Daniel had watched Noah as he went to speak to Ms. Voss. *Quiet confidence,* he thought. He wasn't entirely sure what that was: he'd heard his mom use the phrase to describe one of her friends, but it felt like it applied to Noah too. He seemed so calm, and he didn't need to have a crowd of people around him egging him on. Daniel glanced around at the other students. He was already beginning to like them. He also liked the school, which was new and clean—and so far, the teachers were really nice. He wished with his whole heart that his parents would permanently settle down here in this pretty neighborhood and let him make real friends for once.

He thought to himself, *If I get onto the soccer team, and we win the championship, maybe Mom and Dad will let us stay. It can't hurt. I'll join the team and do my best.*

Daniel's attention sharpened on Noah and Ms. Voss. It seemed she was asking him about the thing on his head. Noah smiled and shook his head, and that seemed to make Ms. Voss happy. He again wondered what it was, then shrugged off the thought. If they were going to be on the team together, he'd have plenty of time to find out all about Noah.

Ms. Voss dismissed the new class to head off to the shower. She sighed deeply as she looked over the list of hopefuls who'd put their names down to join the team. She thought, *How many of them will drop out after the first session when they realize the team is the laughingstock of the whole area? We've lost every single game in two years. They've only scored three goals in all that time.*

In the meantime, Noah would have been surprised to realize that Daniel had even noticed him. When gym was over, he had signed up for the team, grabbed the permission form, and quickly headed to the locker room to claim his place on the far side, right against the wall.

The other boys forged ahead while Daniel lingered a while, hoping to talk with Noah. They walked out together, and Daniel saw the strange thing on Noah's head again.

"Hi," said Daniel. "You're Noah, right?"

"Hi," Noah replied a little awkwardly. "And you're Daniel." His cochlear implant squawked, and he automatically reached up to adjust it.

"Yeah," said Daniel, watching Noah. "Can I ask . . . what is that?"

"This?" Noah was usually uncomfortable when people asked him about his cochlear implant, but Daniel was so straightforward, interested, and friendly, that he found he didn't mind. "It's a cochlear implant." Seeing Daniel's brows draw together in confusion, he continued, "I was born almost completely deaf, and hearing aids don't work for me. This is implanted into my ear, and it stimulates the cochlea, which is a part of the ear that helps with hearing."

"Cool," said Daniel. "So you can hear OK now?"

"Not really," Noah said with a shrug. "I don't know what sound is like for you. The implant lets me pick up signals that I've learned to understand are sounds, like words and stuff. But it's probably not exactly the same as you hear."

Daniel's frowned deepened.

Noah laughed a little. "Don't worry about it. The short answer is, yes, it helps me to hear. But if you talk to me when I'm not looking at you and I don't answer, I'm not being rude, I probably just don't realize you're talking to me."

"OK." Daniel smiled. "I'll make sure I've got your attention."

"I bet you will," Noah said sarcastically, but with a grin.

Daniel's eyes widened and his mouth fell open. "Oh!" he exclaimed. "Is that how it's going to be?"

"Sure is." Noah grinned, suddenly feeling very happy. Mom had been right, it seemed. He actually had made a friend on his first day at the new school, and it eased his nerves a little. They sat beside each other in their next class, and in between the science experiments they were doing in pairs, Noah confided that his parents were super protective over him because of the deafness, always hovering, always worrying.

Daniel listened sympathetically, and in turn, he explained about his parents and how they were both so wrapped up in their work all the time. He admitted that sometimes he worried they would just forget they had a son. They had once forgotten to come and pick him up from school for an embarrassingly long forty minutes while Daniel's grumpy teacher had phoned them both, leaving annoyed voice messages. Noah's eyes widened, and for a fleeting moment, he was grateful for his parents' fussiness—he had never felt unimportant to them. If anything, he felt *too* important to them, as though *their* happiness was dependent on *him* being happy. On the other hand, Daniel thought about Noah's parents hovering over him, assessing all his hobbies and activities before letting him do anything. He had a rare moment of being grateful for all the freedom that came along with the absence of his parents. He could come and go as he pleased so long as he was home by bedtime.

But both boys wished their parents could be just a little bit like the other's—just the smallest amount!

#23

chapter #2

The Terrible Team

BY SATURDAY, neither Daniel nor Noah was looking forward to their first soccer training session. The boys in gym class who'd been laughing had explained to them that the team was the worst in the area, so Noah and Daniel's delight was somewhat diminished. The classmates had crowed that the few good players the team once had had chosen to go to a neighboring club that "actually has a chance of winning a game sometime this century!"

Noah felt miserable, too miserable to even try faking a smile as he slouched toward the soccer field. He had an older half-brother, Gabriel, who came to visit their dad once or twice a year. He lived with his own mom the rest of the time. Gabriel and Dad got along really well, and they often watched soccer on TV before playing soccer in the yard together. Noah always wanted to join them, but Gabriel was so good at the sport that Noah had always hung back, preferring them to think he wasn't interested at all. Gabriel was on a local team—one of the really good ones that the other boys had mentioned. Noah couldn't help but feel humiliated, as though the team's poor quality was a deliberate joke at his expense. He could imagine his parents sitting him down, their expressions concerned as they asked him why he had joined such a useless team and saying he had nothing to prove to them. They might say if he couldn't play well enough to join a good team, perhaps he shouldn't play at all.

Walking next to him, in just as poor a mood, Daniel was also brooding. *My parents will hear about the terrible team,* he thought gloomily, *and move even faster than they usually do.* He'd probably be signed up for another new school within a month at this rate.

They walked toward the soccer field, their steps slowing down more, the closer they got. Neither of them realized they were feeling the same way about it all. As they were both at the point of turning to the other to say, "I can't do this," footsteps sounded behind them. Ms. Voss and a boy Noah recognized from class jogged up to them.

"Hi, Noah, hi, Daniel," said Ms. Voss. "You're a little late, but that's OK. I am too, so I'll let us all off just this once." She gave them both a big wink.

Noah and Daniel smiled politely at the feeble joke and allowed her to usher them onto the field in front of her. They had no idea that Ms. Voss knew exactly how they were feeling. But she wasn't going to let them get away without giving the team a trial, seeing as they were already here.

"Please get the balls, son," she said to the boy who'd jogged with her.

"Sure, Mom." The boy turned to Noah and Daniel. "I'm Benji. Ms. Voss is my mom. Can you give me a hand?"

"Sure." Daniel shrugged and followed Benji. Noah tagged along too, thinking he might as well make himself useful.

Ms. Voss gathered the team around her and gave them a pep talk filled with phrases like, "Try your best" and "Winning isn't the only goal." She tried for a team cheer, but the response was so ragged and disheartened that she quickly moved on to placing them in groups to perform basic soccer drills. Having paired up, Daniel and Noah

looked around and saw, to their horror, that the team was even worse than they could have imagined! Even in pairs, just kicking back and forth, the balls were rolling wildly all over the field. Ms. Voss moved from group to group, advising and pointing, but Noah couldn't see anyone improving at all, even a tiny bit.

By the end of practice, Ms. Voss had kept her determined smile in place as she let everyone go off to shower and head home.

Noah and Daniel had discovered they lived close to one another, so they walked together. On the way, they dodged the topic of soccer. Instead, they talked about Daniel's favorite school that he'd been to; the funniest thing Noah's parents had done to protect him; and their rather challenging math homework neither of them had attempted yet.

The next practice was on Tuesday, after school.

That day, at lunchtime, Noah said to Daniel, "I'm thinking about not going to the soccer club anymore."

Daniel turned to him with relief. "Oh, thank goodness! It's so bad, right?"

"Terrible!" Noah exclaimed. "What excuse can we give for not going?"

"Um . . ." Daniel thought about it. "We could say someone died."

"No." Noah shook his head. "I wouldn't feel good about that."

"No, you're right," agreed Daniel. "Uh—you could get sick? Then I could walk you home."

"That's a thought," Noah replied. He rubbed his chin with a hand. "But can we make it so *you're* sick and I go with you? If my parents find out I said I was sick, they'll check me into the hospital for tests for two weeks!"

"Sure," said Daniel. "I'll have . . ."

But before Daniel could decide on which illness to choose, Benji walked by and suddenly stopped. His normally friendly, laughing face was serious.

"Guys," he begged. "Please don't give up. Give the team a chance."

"But it's terrible," Noah moaned. "It's embarrassing."

"Sure." Benji crossed his arms over his chest. "And people come along for one practice, see how bad it is, and then never come back. So the club never ever gets better, and everyone just makes fun of it. How can it get better if no one ever gives it a chance?"

"Well, I'm not even very good myself," Noah said feebly. "I'll just make things worse."

"I don't know." Daniel shrugged. "I'll see how I feel later."

Benji looked at them for a moment longer then turned away. The disappointment on his face made both Daniel and Noah feel guilty—but not quite guilty enough to commit to going to practice later that day.

"Come to my place after school," Noah suggested. "My Grandpa Hugo lives next door and I'm going over there. He'll make us something to eat, and then we can play out back. He's got a huge yard; it's so much fun."

"Sounds good," Daniel replied happily. Usually, he had to make his own snack after school, as his mom and dad would be working in their separate little offices, the doors tightly shut so they could concentrate. It meant that he could watch whatever he wanted to, but it was also lonely sometimes. It would be nice to have some company—and to have an adult make his snack for a change.

The two of them knocked at Grandpa Hugo's door later that day.

"Hello, Noah!" Grandpa Hugo greeted, happy to see his youngest grandson at the door. "Oh, I see! Double trouble today, huh? And who's this young man?"

"Grandpa Hugo, this is Daniel," Noah explained politely. "We're in the same class."

"Well, the more the merrier." Grandpa Hugo solemnly shook Daniel's hand, smiled, and ushered them into his big, cool kitchen. "I'm sure you're both hungry. How about . . ." He glanced around his kitchen, one bony finger to his mouth as he pondered. "I can do chocolate, strawberry, or banana milkshakes—made with *real bananas*!" He raised his eyebrows at them comically, making them both laugh. "And," he continued, "sandwiches with ham, cheese, tomato, or any combination you want, grilled or otherwise. What are we having?"

They quickly settled on strawberry milkshakes with toasted ham, cheese, and tomato sandwiches. With all three of them working together, they were sitting at Grandpa Hugo's small dining table, eating, not too long after.

As Daniel ate, politely remembering to take small bites and chew with his mouth closed (he sometimes didn't bother with good manners when he was eating alone), he flicked careful glances at Noah and his grandpa. They were easy in each other's company, clearly used to spending a lot of time together, and chatted without worry. He noticed that Noah didn't mind having his cochlear implant on his grandpa's side. He had picked up on Noah's tendency to keep that side against the wall whenever he was around unfamiliar people or large crowds. Grandpa Hugo seemed curious about Daniel. He asked Daniel a series of questions about himself, his interests, his parents and their work. Daniel rambled away, liking Grandpa Hugo's easy way, and envying Noah's close relationship with the white-bearded old man.

As their sandwiches were reduced to crumbs, Grandpa Hugo turned his attention to Noah, who had listened carefully to their chatter. He asked, "So, what are you doing this afternoon?"

"Oh," Noah started as he used a finger to pick up toast crumbs from his plate, "I thought Daniel and I would play in the yard if that's OK. We can make a fort down at the bottom with some of those old sheets of particleboard."

"Sure, no problem," Grandpa Hugo replied. "Boys should always have a place to be boys, but don't you have soccer today? I'm sure your mom said soccer on Tuesdays, Thursdays, and Saturdays."

"Uh . . ." Noah went pink and looked a bit guilty.

Daniel glanced down at his plate and slurped a mouthful of milkshake.

"We were, like . . . not going to go today," Noah admitted.

"But you like soccer!" Grandpa Hugo sounded surprised. "You practiced all summer and begged your mom to be allowed to join, didn't you?"

"I do like it, but honestly, Grandpa, the team is terrible. There are no good players, us included. Everyone's so bad!"

"Rosie's good," Daniel added fairly.

"Yeah, Rosie's good," agreed Noah. "And Benji's not bad, either. But there's no one as good as Gabriel. The team's useless and has lost every game for two whole years!"

Grandpa Hugo looked at Noah. He wasn't scowling and he still had a slight smile on his face, but the boys immediately understood that he was disappointed with them.

Noah tried to explain, "Grandpa, boys laughed when we said we wanted to join the team! If we stick with it, they'll laugh at *us* next." Noah glanced at Daniel who just nodded to show his agreement. Noah continued, "I'm not brave enough to get laughed at."

Grandpa Hugo looked from one to the other again, and now his gaze was warmer, more sympathetic. "Boys," he said softly, "courage isn't just about fearing something. It's about fearing it and doing it anyway. I hope you'd rather be thought brave than not."

He didn't wait for a reply as he stood to gather their empty plates. The boys finished their milkshakes and brought the glasses to the sink.

Then they sat back at the kitchen table, both feeling miserable and unhappy. But slowly, it dawned on both of them that what they were feeling miserable about wasn't the thought of *going* to soccer practice. It was the thought of *not* going.

Noah glanced at Daniel and saw he was already looking back at him steadily.

"We're going, aren't we?" Noah asked, feeling a weight lift off his heart.

"We're going," agreed Daniel with a sheepish grin. "For better or for worse, we're going."

"Ew." Noah grinned. "I'm not marrying you!"

Laughing, Daniel pretend-punched Noah's arm as they gathered up their school things to leave in a tidy pile by the door until after practice, and then went off to change for soccer.

As they walked onto the field, they were both regretting their decision to come, especially as they saw how few of the other new sign-ups had arrived.

"I really don't feel very brave," Daniel muttered to Noah.

"I hear that," Noah replied quietly as they approached Ms. Voss.

"Daniel! Noah!" Ms. Voss sounded genuinely delighted to see them and a little surprised too. Noah glanced at Benji and saw a mixture of happiness for them and relief for his mom on his face.

"Actually," Daniel said as they jogged to their positions on the field, "I'm glad we did come."

"Yeah," said Noah. "Me too."

chapter 3

Making the Best of It

BUT THEIR RELIEF didn't last very long. As poor as the other team members' skills were, Daniel and Noah were horrified to realize they were just as bad. They found their coordination left a lot to be desired. Daniel could kick powerfully, but not accurately, and Noah's kicks went straight, but not very far. Passing was a nightmare too. They spent more time running to retrieve the ball than passing it to one another. And neither of them could dribble reliably for more than three steps at a time. They became breathless after just a few minutes of running around.

Their embarrassment made them grumpy, and soon, they were fighting.

"Kick straight! Geez!" yelled Noah.

"I am!" Daniel snapped. "Run faster, slowpoke!"

"Noah, Daniel, what's going on here?" Ms. Voss heard the commotion and came over to investigate.

They both tried to loudly explain their problems, neither letting the other speak. Ms. Voss pulled out her whistle and blew a sharp note on it. They stopped talking and stared at her.

"You're getting frustrated," she explained gently. "Try working together, not against each other. Soccer is all about teamwork, and for that, you need to listen to one another and work with everyone else on the team. I'll get Rosie to come and work with you for a while. She's good at listening and communicating." Ms. Voss raised a hand and waved Rosie over.

She jogged up, her face expressionless, and Noah felt bad for her. He wondered what it was like being the best player of the bunch, and if she felt miserable being the only girl on the team.

"Rosie, Noah and Daniel are struggling with the set moves. Can you watch them for a minute and help them when they go wrong?"

Rosie nodded. "Sure, no problem, Ms. Voss. OK, guys, move closer together and pass the ball. Just gentle kicks, roll the ball to each other."

Ms. Voss smiled gratefully at Rosie before setting off to break up a group of players who seemed to be talking rather than practicing.

"Pfft!" Daniel said. "That's baby stuff!"

"OK," said Rosie. "But you need to master the baby stuff before you try the more advanced stuff."

Daniel was momentarily speechless.

Noah laughed.

"You too!" Rosie said practically. "Neither of you are great at the basics, so let's start with the so-called baby stuff, and if you manage that, we'll move further apart and get to the more advanced stuff, OK?"

Reluctantly, but seeing that Rosie was making a lot of sense, they moved together and rolled the ball to each other. Rosie turned away for a moment to talk to Benji, and Daniel kicked the ball hard and wide.

"Hey!" Noah yelled angrily.

"What are you doing?" Rosie turned back and saw Noah chasing the ball down the field. "I said gently!"

Daniel shrugged grumpily. He had such high hopes of soccer, but he was so bad at it. There was no way his parents would agree to stay put if he was a terrible player.

#39

Noah dribbled the ball back, losing it once or twice, and Rosie rolled her eyes impatiently.

"Come *on*!" she complained. "I didn't ask to be put in charge of you, you know. Don't take it out on me just because I'm a girl! You know what? Go dribble all around the field, as fast as you can!"

Daniel and Noah protested that they were upset with each other, and not with her, but she didn't want to hear it. So they started to run around the field, detouring to recapture the balls that did not want to stay at their toes. Rosie folded her arms, her mouth a narrow line, as she watched their slow progress.

When they made it back to her, she scolded them more about being respectful to those who are just trying to help them. Daniel and Noah again tried to protest their innocence, but they were talking over each other, and Rosie couldn't clearly make out what they were saying.

Just as she was about to lose her temper with them, Benji came running up, followed closely by another boy. "Hey, Rosie, can I say something?"

"What?" she growled, but she moved over to him willingly.

#40

"I don't think they're being jerks on purpose," Benji said. "I think they're worse at the skills than they thought they would be, and that's what they're getting upset about. They're not arguing with you, it's more . . ." He gestured at the soccer field and surrounding school building. ". . . everything!"

"Oh." Rosie calmed down and turned back to look at her charges. Noah was talking enthusiastically to the other boy while Daniel was standing nearby, moodily rolling the ball under one foot while listening to them.

When Rosie had moved away to talk to Benji, Noah glanced at the other boy, and then frowned.

"Don't I know you?" he asked. "We were at elementary school together—maybe kindergarten?"

"Yes!" the boy exclaimed. "I'm Oliver and you're Noah! We were buddies for a while, before we moved away."

"It's so good to see you again!" Noah replied. "Do you remember . . ."

And they were off, talking about people and places that Daniel didn't know. He felt a pang of something like sorrow. He was used to having people know each other but had hoped at this new school he wouldn't have this hollow feeling in his stomach. It was a sense of being an outsider, tolerated but not known. However, in a moment, Noah turned to him, his face bright and happy. He had forgotten their scratchy moments in his joy at seeing his old friend, and it seemed that he still wanted to include Daniel too.

"Daniel, this is Oliver, an old friend. Oliver, this is Daniel, my new friend." Daniel felt a little warm glow at the simple "my new friend" and shook hands with Oliver in a friendly manner. The three of them stood talking together so they could all catch up with their news.

As practice finished, Noah received a text message from Grandpa Hugo.

Grandpa Hugo: Hey kiddo, your parents are out for dinner tonight, so it's soup and toast unless you want to grab takeout.

Noah: Could I maybe go get pizza with friends instead?

Grandpa Hugo: No problem. Be home by 6:30. Got enough money?

Noah: Yes. Mom gave me my allowance today.

Grandpa Hugo: Great, will pay you back when you get in, seeing as I'm meant to feed you :-)

Noah: Thanks, Grandpa. Love you!

Noah looked at Oliver and Daniel. "Want to go get pizza?" he asked, trying to sound casual.

"I'd love to!" Oliver replied promptly.

"Yeah, me too!" added Daniel. "Unless you two want to catch up or something."

"Don't be silly!" Noah said. "Come on, it'll be fun."

Feeling a sense of relief and now cheerful, Daniel sent his parents a message, knowing that if they saw it before he got home, they wouldn't mind. Oliver phoned his parents, and they were happy to hear he had met Noah again and gave him permission to go for pizza. The terrible practice suddenly forgotten, the three of them headed toward the nearby small strip mall that housed a couple of fast-food restaurants, a small grocery store, and a thrift store. At this time on a weekday, the pizzeria was empty, and they chose a big table by the window so they could watch the world go by.

Daniel was slightly surprised when Oliver sat next to him. Throughout their conversation, he realized that whenever Oliver spoke to Noah, he would lower his drink or pizza slice and face Noah directly, speaking very clearly. Daniel wondered about it for a while. But then, when he saw Noah brush down his hair over his cochlear implant in the way that was already familiar to him, he suddenly understood. Oliver was doing it because it helped Noah hear him more clearly. Oliver was so natural about what he was doing that Noah wasn't at all embarrassed about it. In fact, he barely seemed to have noticed it at all. Daniel had seen that Noah sometimes blushed when people asked if he needed any extra help because of his hearing issues, especially if they treated him like a poor creature.

Daniel burned with embarrassment for a moment, kicking himself for not realizing that Noah would need people to be mindful of his deafness, even if they didn't treat him any differently for it. He had even said as much the first time they'd spoken. For a moment, he resented Oliver, as though Oliver's kindness made Daniel's forgetfulness look bad. But then he calmed down, seeing the happiness on Noah's face as he looked from one to the other.

I'll be just like Oliver from now on, Daniel promised himself. *I'll be considerate too.* He turned his attention to what Oliver was saying and realized he was telling a story about something funny that had happened when he was on vacation with his parents. Apparently, a fish had swum right up Oliver's dad's trunks, causing him to scream and jump around. No one could understand what had happened for a long time and therefore couldn't help him remove the fishy intruder.

Noah laughed so hard that tears ran down his face. Daniel ate his pizza, conscious of feeling left out—but also aware that he didn't need to be feeling this way. Noah was trying to include Daniel in the conversation, explaining the names that popped up in Oliver's stories, and glancing at him, waiting for a shared reaction. Daniel shook off the feeling of being the outsider. Oliver mentioned a vacation when his family had gone snorkeling, and how cool it was seeing the fish and other sea creatures.

This gave Daniel the opportunity to share his own story. His family had lived in a hotel near the sea for a short while. He recounted the story of a man who dove into the ocean but lost his swimsuit. He had stayed under the water, his face bright pink with shame, until he managed to get the attention of one of the hotel staff, who had brought him a towel to protect his modesty.

"But," added Daniel with a grin, "later on, we saw the hotel server howling with laughter with his manager about it. They kept trying to stop laughing but then their eyes would meet, and they would laugh again." While he spoke, Daniel remembered to keep his pizza slice below the level of his mouth and to keep his face turned more toward Noah. Noah listened carefully and laughed in all the right places. Daniel was pleased to see that his usual little squint of concentration had eased too.

Happy with himself, Daniel asked Noah, "What about you? Any funny vacation stories to share?"

"Yeah," Oliver said in between laughs. "Your turn."

"I . . ." Noah thought for a moment. There were some funny stories to share. There was the Russian family who had accidentally been given the wrong room key: a duplicate of Noah's family's hotel room. The Russians walked in on Noah's family sprawled in front of the big television, all pink and peeling after a day in the blazing sun. Or there was the time Dad had accidentally left the bath running in their hotel room which meant they'd come back to a complete flood throughout the entire suite. And, of course, who could forget that polite Frenchman who had been convinced that Noah's mom was his ex-girlfriend despite the large age difference, the fact that she had never visited the town the man was talking about, and that she had only ever dated his dad.

Noah thought about which story to begin with and tried to think up a good, snappy beginning. He racked his brain, but everything he thought of saying seemed silly and mean, so he ended up not saying anything at all. He shook his head, closed his eyes, and took a bite of his pizza, as though it was the most delicious thing ever. When he opened his eyes, he saw Daniel was looking thoughtfully at him, but neither of them said anything.

This was unfortunate, because Daniel thought Noah was grumpy with him for taking over Oliver's storytelling. Daniel knew he tended to push himself forward. It was a result of his parents not really seeming to see him. But sometimes, people thought he was rude because of it, so he was trying very hard to make sure he didn't steal all the limelight. The three boys fell into a slightly awkward silence as they each finished their pizza, leaving nothing but small crumbs on the plates. But the awkwardness was jolted when Noah casually glanced at his watch, then bolted to his feet.

"Oh gosh, it's late! We'd better go, or we'll be in trouble. I will, anyway. They'll ground me for a month!"

They hurried to tidy the table before racing home, Oliver peeling off to head toward his own house with a wave as he went. The rushed walk-jog home seemed to have dispelled the awkwardness, and Noah said, "Good night, see you tomorrow," to Daniel with a smile.

"See ya," Daniel called, slowing down once Noah was inside his yard. *Mom and Dad won't worry about me for at least another hour,* he thought to himself. He watched Noah jog to the door, where he was greeted by his mom. Noah pointed out Daniel standing by the gate, and Noah's mom waved in a friendly manner. Then she ushered Noah inside and shut the door behind them. Thoughtfully, Daniel headed for home and was proved correct in his assumption: neither of his parents asked where he had been but did pause their work for a few minutes to talk with him.

On Thursday, their language arts teacher asked the class if anyone knew what a palindrome was. Daniel, listening obediently, shook his head like most of the class. But he saw an urgent look on Noah's face. He saw how Noah seemed to be wanting to raise his hand but was wrestling with himself. Daniel couldn't encourage Noah to go for it without the rest of the class—and worse, the teacher—hearing him, but he tried to mentally will Noah to do it. But it was too late. The moment had passed, and when no one could tell her the answer, she set it as part of their homework to find out. Daniel had just finished writing down the rest of his homework when the bell rang for recess, and he and Noah headed outside. He noticed that Noah was looking a bit moody again, just as he had at the pizza shop.

"Noah?" Daniel asked the question in his usual blunt and unfiltered way. "Did you know the answer but felt scared about speaking up?"

Noah turned to him and opened his mouth to reply, but Daniel continued.

"And is that why you didn't tell us any funny vacation stories yesterday?"

Noah's mouth slammed shut, and he glared at Daniel.

"Because you shouldn't worry about anything, you know. Just talk! No one will laugh or mock you, and you have to learn to communicate better, don't you?"

Daniel didn't realize that his words sounded as though they were aimed at Noah: he didn't intend them that way. Rather, he meant, "We all have to learn to communicate better as we grow up"—but he didn't communicate that very effectively *at all*!

As a result, Noah heard his new friend seeming to

scold him for allowing his deafness to keep him quiet when he shouldn't.

Noah's normally calm mood flared, and he snapped at Daniel. "Well, maybe," he growled, "I would speak up if anyone else ever gave me a chance! Maybe it's not my deafness, maybe it's you!"

Daniel was horrified. "Oh, no! Noah! I didn't mean . . . I only said . . . "

"Oh, whatever!" Noah gathered the books he needed for his next class and ran off to line up early outside the classroom. It wasn't a class that Daniel was in, so he couldn't follow him and force Noah to see sense. *He's being so sensitive,* Daniel thought, heaving an irritated sigh. He went to sit outside his next class, his face the picture of gloom.

Daniel thought about skipping out on the soccer club that afternoon but decided not to in the end. He was secretly hoping they would be put back into pairs. A couple of hours of passing to each other would hopefully be enough to give Noah time to apologize to him. Then Daniel could explain what he'd actually meant.

But Ms. Voss had a different idea for practice today. She divided them into two teams—doing it herself so no one was left to the last, then gave one side red vests to put over their shirts.

"We're going to play a game today," she said happily. "I think actually playing the game, instead of just running drills all the time, will make us feel better. Plus, it'll be fun!"

It wasn't fun. It wasn't fun at all! Noah and Daniel were on opposite teams, and Ms. Voss had placed them in positions that meant they never came close to each other. Both of them kept looking at the other to see what they were doing and what kind of a mood they seemed to be in, but they both assumed the other was glaring at them in anger. As a result, they both played poorly, missing easy passes, kicking badly, or simply not paying attention to the game. The rest of the team wasn't much better, and soon Ms. Voss's whistle was sounding over and over again as she tried to calm fraying tempers and keep the game moving. The ball flew off the field in every direction except for that of the goal, with each poor kick or pass causing that player to receive angry shouts.

Finally, Ms. Voss ran into the middle of the field and blew her whistle loudly and repeatedly to end the game.

Everyone was used to Ms. Voss being kind and calm, no matter what happened at practice, so it was a surprise for everyone to realize she was upset with them.

#51

"That was terrible," she said. "No one listens to anyone else. You each think you are the one who should end up with the ball. Every single one of you was telling everyone else what to do instead of doing it yourself! That is, if you could be bothered to pay attention to the game for more than a minute at a time!"

When she said this last comment, she gave Noah and Daniel a quick, grumpy glance and they realized they had drawn closer to each other when she asked everyone to huddle up.

"You all need to learn to listen, first of all," she said, her voice calming down to her usual tone. "And you all need to think about what the team needs, instead of what you, personally, *want*. Soccer is a team sport. It's not every player for themselves." She looked around at her ragged team and stifled a sigh. "And also, when you're talking to each other, take the time to listen to the others and understand why they're saying what they are. I saw so many opportunities wasted because no one listened when players yelled to say they were free. OK, go on, shower and head home. I'll see you on Saturday."

As they headed to the locker room, Noah remembered Daniel trying to explain something to him when they'd argued earlier.

But at the same time, Daniel was thinking over his words, and he realized that Noah could have taken them as criticism, rather than advice.

They turned to each other at the same time and spoke in perfect unison. "I'm sorry, I didn't—" And just like that, they were laughing again, the best of friends, and more than ready to make up from that morning.

After they changed, they walked home together as usual. Daniel took the opportunity to explain what he'd meant. Noah let him know how it had sounded, and they soon settled the matter between them. Their conversation then turned to the much more serious topic of the team and just how very bad it was. But they also talked about how it could be improved and how each of them could play their own part in creating that success.

chapter 4

Not Good Enough!

PRETTY SOON, the five most dedicated soccer players began to hang out together at recess and lunch: Rosie and Benji were already good friends, and they accepted the small group of Noah, Daniel, and Oliver too—especially when they realized that they really wanted to help the soccer team improve. Rosie told Daniel and Noah that if they all did some extra practice, the team would have five decent players. She added that, between them, they should be able to help the weaker players. As a result, Noah, Daniel, and Oliver spent every spare moment practicing or thinking up how to better their corner kicks, penalties, and goal kicks. They spent some of their class and homework time on the task too.

Noah got home one day and found himself at the dining table, a concerned parent on either side of him.

"Noah," his mom began, "Dad and I are very worried about you. We just got a call from your principal."

"Oh?" Noah was confused. He hadn't been in any trouble at school. *What on earth could this be about?*

"Your grades have been slipping," his dad said. "*Alarmingly*, the principal said. What's going on? Are you being bullied?"

"Oh, no!" Noah replied after thinking about it. "I guess . . . I've been thinking so much about the soccer team and how we can make it better. I might have forgotten about some of my homework."

Mom's eyebrows drew together. "Noah," she said sternly. "I know you love your soccer buddies, but your schoolwork is the most important thing."

Dad nodded solemnly. "Your mom's right, Noah. We're glad it's nothing more serious, but you need to get good grades, OK? It's important for your future. The more work you put in now, the easier things will be for you as a grown-up."

Noah nodded. In all honesty, he had never really been scolded by his parents before, and he was finding it to be an intriguing experience. But he soon started to pay attention when his mom said he had three months to get his grades up to a good level, or else they would take away his permission to be a part of the soccer club.

"Wait, what?" Noah had never been refused permission for social activities because of his behavior before. It was usually his deafness or the implant that decided whether he could do something.

"You heard me," his mom added. "We love that you've made friends and joined the team. We can see it's done a lot for your confidence. But you need a good academic base before you need friends or soccer. So, that's the deal. Get your grades up to an A average in three months, or no more soccer club."

Noah knew there was no arguing with his parents when they had a united front, so he swallowed hard and nodded, agreeing to their terms.

Around the corner, Daniel, too, found himself in an unusual position. His parents had come to his bedroom. It was an event so unusual that he immediately thought they were about to move again, even though they had barely unpacked all their things after the last one. But they sat on his bed, facing him at the small desk he used for homework—and also for planning soccer plays, as he was doing now.

"Stop doing that a minute," Dad said, glancing at Mom to see if she would take the lead.

"Just for a bit," she replied softly. "We got a phone call from your school. Your grades are below where they need to be. Something about rushed homework to do extra soccer practice or something?"

Daniel nodded, half-wishing his parents would go back to their usual loving neglect of him, half-wishing they did *this* more often. Come in and talk seriously to him about, well, about *anything* really. "Yes," he managed. "The team isn't great, but there are a few of us trying to improve it so we . . . like . . . don't finish last in the league."

Mom twisted her wrist to peep at the time, and Daniel knew he wouldn't have her attention for much longer: she was on a deadline, once again.

He went on, quickly, "So, yeah, maybe my schoolwork has dipped a bit."

"Reverse that dip," Dad said, the mild tone softening the harsh words. "Your principal said that unless your little group sorts itself out, he might ban you all from playing on the team."

Daniel's mouth sagged open in shock. "He can't!"

"He can," corrected Mom. "And if your schoolwork doesn't return to its usual level, we'll let him."

Daniel transferred his outrage from the absent principal to his present mom, staring at her with his mouth still open.

"You'll catch flies." Dad was trying to hide a smile. "It's a simple ask, son. Stay on top of your work, and we'll leave your soccer alone. Deal?"

Daniel recovered himself enough to manage a nod and croaked, "Deal."

Pleased, Dad ruffled his hair while Mom gave him a swift hug. They exited his room, leaving him still faintly stunned. The teachers hadn't even warned them or anything. Muttering to himself, Daniel slipped his hand under his pillow and retrieved his phone. As he was thinking about what to write in the soccer team group chat, it vibrated in his hand.

Noah: My grades are down. Mom + Dad not happy. Must fix or no soccer!!!

Benji: Me too. Mom mad. She won't make me give up soccer (she knows I'd just take music instead!) but I have to figure it out. Ugh!

#58

Oliver: And me! Folks are really mad. I'm grounded but can come to soccer. Have to get better grades or else!

Daniel: Even my parents were told! The principal called them! And same, have to do better.

As they sat in their various bedrooms, the boys noticed that one of their group members hadn't messaged about being put on notice if their grades didn't improve.

Noah: @Rosie? You in trouble too?

Rosie: Nope! I don't let my grades fall. I'm not all that clever, I have to work hard to do well.

Noah: How though!?? I thought I was doing my usual schoolwork!

Rosie: No you weren't. You spend most of your homework time talking about soccer and discussing the other team members. Scroll back through the chat, you'll see!

Benji: Don't bother, Rosie's right. I already checked.

#59

Noah: Well, what are we going to do? I don't want to have to leave the team. Even if we're terrible!

Rosie: I dunno. Gotta go, chat tomorrow at practice?

Noah: I guess . . .

But Daniel and Noah didn't go to practice. Depressed by their schoolwork slipping, suddenly secretly convinced that all their hard work was for nothing and thinking the team would never get any better, they decided to skip. They didn't tell anyone, just slinking off after school and going straight to Grandpa Hugo's house.

Grandpa Hugo welcomed them as before, and this time, he seemed to sense the boys were too upset to be lectured about their responsibilities to the team. Instead, he let them sit at his dining room table and start working on their homework. He even helped them when they both declared they had no idea how to solve one of the sets of math problems, showing them where they were going wrong. The afternoon and early evening flew by, and if Noah or Daniel gave any thought at all to their teammates slogging their way through exercises and skills, neither of them said it out loud.

But the next morning, Ms. Voss came to find them just as they were deciding what to do for recess.

"Daniel! Noah!" Ms. Voss stalked up to them, her disappointment clear in every word. "May I have a word with you please? In here." She opened the door to an empty classroom and shooed them in, standing with her back to the door so they would not be able to escape. "Why did neither of you come to practice yesterday? And why was your absence not explained to me in any form: you could have phoned or texted me; you could have emailed me; you could have left a message with reception. Heck, you could have just let Benji know and asked him to tell me."

Noah and Daniel exchanged a glance, and then both stared at the ground in front of them. They hadn't thought about letting Ms. Voss know, not for a single moment.

"Sorry, Ms. Voss," whispered Noah. "We didn't think."

They weren't going to be let off lightly. "It was extremely rude of you," Ms. Voss went on. "And you might not have realized this—in fact, I really hope you *haven't* realized this, as if you knew and still flaked out on me." They both winced at the harsh words, but neither could protest that it wasn't true. "That would just make *this*," she waved her hand at them, "so much worse!"

She took a deep breath, visibly tried to calm herself, and started again. "Since you two joined the team, everything has started to come together. It's as though two more fairly decent players joining the team gave them all new hope. But yesterday, when you just weren't there and no one knew why, the heart went out of them again. It was a terrible practice, perhaps the worst I've ever seen. And believe me, I've seen some stinkers. When you join a team, boys, you assume responsibility for the team *and* your teammates. You let me down yesterday; you let the team down; but most of all, you let yourselves down. I'm really, *really* disappointed in you both." Ms. Voss spun on her heel and exited the classroom, leaving the door swinging open as she turned right, heading for the staff room.

Stunned, Noah turned to Daniel. "We should have said why we weren't coming."

"I guess," Daniel replied with a shrug. "I feel even worse now, though. How are we going to face the others?" He scoffed. "But I guess that's not really going to be a problem. My parents will move in about a week, and I'll never see any of you again."

"And my half-brother will come over and keep being the one my dad talks to about soccer," added Noah. "We might as well give up now and never play soccer again."

"Excuse me?" Rosie's voice was loud and indignant. "What are you talking about? You're not giving up on the team, not now. We're just starting to get better!"

"Oh, Rosie." Noah sighed. "What's the point? I'm a loser. I can't play soccer and can't keep up with my schoolwork. Daniel's parents will probably move them all in a few months, so he'll be gone too."

Daniel nodded gloomily. "We're not driven like you are, Rosie," he added. "I don't know how you do it."

"I'll help you," she volunteered. "I'll show you how to manage soccer practice without letting your grades slip."

They looked at her, their expressions a mixture of surprise and hope.

"How?" Noah asked.

"I'll make schedules for you," she explained. "Like the one I made for myself." She looked at them, a scowl on her face. "But if I do all this work for you and you let me down, or get yourselves kicked off the team, or . . . or . . . cause *my* grades to fall, there will be *consequences*!" She stomped a foot for added effect.

Neither one of them wanted to ask what she meant by consequences. Her tone of voice let them know they would not be pleasant, and that was enough of a reason to not get on her bad side.

"Thanks, Rosie," Daniel said genuinely. "We do appreciate it, honestly."

Noah nodded his agreement.

Rosie glared at them, then her face softened into a smile. "It's going to be hard work, but honestly, it's kind of fun too, making sure you get everything done in time. Send me your schedules, and I'll make catch-up timetables, ready to start tomorrow after school."

The next day, she handed each of them a piece of paper with a week neatly laid out across the whole page.

"Whoa!" Noah exclaimed. "You even included my speech therapy!"

"Of course," Rosie said with a smile. "It's important, plus you said you needed to go."

"And my Saturday mornings with Dad!" Daniel added happily. He scanned the rest of the page. "But wow, there's not a lot of spare time, is there?"

"Well," she started, "you have two choices: you can use my schedule, which gets you all caught up with your schoolwork, and then keeps you up-to-date, and gives you plenty of soccer time, but not a lot of 'free time.'" She hooked her fingers into air quotes as she spoke. "Or you can let everything slide so your parents do move you to a new place, where you won't know anyone or be part of any clubs, but you'll have all the free time you could want. Your choice, Daniel. What do you think?"

Daniel looked at her nervously. "I think," he started delicately, "your schedule is absolutely perfect. Thank you so much, Rosie. You're a star, my hero, my caped crusader!"

Rosie stuck out her tongue at him, and suddenly they were the best of friends again, their stresses and worries erased by Rosie's careful planning and kindness.

After Rosie left, Daniel confided in Noah. "You know when Rosie said I could just leave for another new school?"

Noah nodded. "Uh-huh."

"I don't want that," Daniel said. "I want to stay here. I want to have a birthday party here with all my new friends. I like it here."

Noah nodded sympathetically. As they went into the classroom, Daniel followed his friend, knowing that as honest as he had been, the truth was so much more than his words had allowed him to say. He was desperate to stay here, in this new, friendly school, living in the clean and well-ordered neighborhood, with friends who had similar interests. The thought of leaving it all behind was crushing.

Rosie hadn't been kidding when she told them it would be hard, but they were both determined to succeed. Knowing she had used her own schedule to maintain her good grades and her interests helped the boys. This was especially the case in the early days when it seemed cruel to have to miss the latest episode of their favorite television show to work on extra math exercises, but their grades stopped their slow decline and began to return to an acceptable level.

To their delight, their fitness on the sports field also improved. Soon, they could easily run a mile without losing their breath. Instead of breathlessly longing for Ms. Voss to blow the whistle for them to go and shower, they found the end of practice coming as a surprise to them. Though they hardly realized it at the time—they were both working far too hard to think about such things—these days were some of the happiest either of them had ever experienced.

chapter 5

Gabriel Comes to Stay

WHEN NOAH'S mom told him Gabriel was coming to stay for a while, Noah felt a weird squirm in his stomach. Gabriel usually came to visit for a week or so whenever his own school allowed, to spend some time with the dad they shared. But this year, Gabriel's mom had taken him traveling for months, and Noah had been able to settle into his new school and make friends without having to face his usual battle with his emotions. But any hopes Noah had that his older half-brother wouldn't have the usual effect on him were in vain. Just hearing Gabriel's name was enough for Noah's stomach to start clenching and churning. And the long time since their last meeting, coupled with everything that had happened to Noah in the meantime—new school, new friends, joining the soccer club—didn't help either.

To make matters worse, Noah's cochlear implant chose today of all days to start acting up, making embarrassingly loud squeaks and feedback whines for no apparent reason. Humiliated, Noah ate his supper quickly and asked to be excused to go do homework. But, for once, he ignored Rosie's carefully written instructions and spent the time trying to adjust his implant. It worked enough for Noah to make out the sounds coming through the wall from the television: the roar of an eager home crowd, the shrill whistle of the referee, and the exclamations and shouts from his dad and half-brother as they urged their soccer team toward the goal.

Finally, the weird noises from his implant stopped, and Noah could turn his attention to his homework. But it still wasn't catching his attention—the soccer game in the next room was the only thing he was aware of.

Telling himself he could work on it in the morning, Noah packed away his homework and stood from his desk. With the intention of joining them watching TV, he planned out how to do it. Normally, he didn't care about Dad and Gabriel watching soccer together. But now that he had begun to play the game himself (even if the team was awful), he really wanted to be included by them. Noah stretched his hand out to open his bedroom door, and at exactly that moment, Daniel knocked at the

#69

front door. Spotting him through the window, Noah ran to answer, suddenly delighted that his best friend was there. As they were discussing what to do, the game on the television went to halftime and Gabriel came out to see who had arrived.

They seemed to size each other up immediately. Gabriel stood as tall as he could—something Noah had noticed he did on the rare occasions he felt ill-at-ease—while Daniel seemed to bristle like an angry cat. Noah wondered if they would have fought with each other if they had been anywhere else. With Gabriel visiting his part-time home, and Daniel being a welcome guest too, neither wanted to make the first move. As it stood, neither one was willing to cave to the other; instead, they just stared each other down.

It was the match starting up again, and Dad yelling for Gabriel to come back into the room, which broke the spell. Gabriel silently joined him, and Daniel and Noah went outside to practice feints and weaves.

They didn't talk much, and Noah couldn't tell what Daniel was thinking. But they had fun passing the ball to each other and were just beginning to relax when Gabriel came out into the yard—urged by Dad to "play with the boys." Reluctantly, Gabriel came toward them,

and Daniel feinted passing the ball to Noah, but instead booted it hard at Gabriel. Completely unfazed (and Noah having fallen for the feint himself), Gabriel took the ball on his chest and allowed it to drop onto his foot. He then proceeded to keep it off the ground with his feet, head, shoulders, and even his back, for several long and excruciating minutes. Daniel had wanted to humiliate Gabriel, but instead found embarrassment. Gabriel, on the other hand, seemed not to even notice the two boys, his entire focus on the ball which he was completely dominating.

Daniel's dilemma turned his face brick red, and he turned to Noah and muttered, "Let's get out of here."

Noah, understanding *exactly* what Daniel was feeling, nodded. After all, he had felt it himself at least once every single time Gabriel had come to stay. He called over his shoulder to Gabriel, "Keep it warm for us. We're just going to the..." He let his words fade, knowing Gabriel wouldn't really care where they were going. Soon, he and Daniel were pedaling hard, enjoying the rush of the wind in their hair and the feeling of freedom. Finally tiring, they slowed down. Daniel got straight to the point.

"What is your half-brother's deal? Why did he have to show off like that?"

"I know!" Noah groaned. "He's always like that. It doesn't matter what I'm doing, he has to come along and do it better all the time. It's really . . ."

"I bet!" Daniel pedaled along for a moment. "You know, I always thought that having a big brother would be cool. But now . . ." He shook his head. "What a jerk."

"Yeah." Noah felt another squirm in his stomach. Gabriel didn't mean to upset him, Noah knew that. "He's just always . . . better looking, really good at school, and . . ." Noah had never admitted this to anyone before, not even his mom or Grandpa Hugo. "I'm sure my dad likes him better. I mean . . . why wouldn't he? Look at me, compared to Gabriel."

"I prefer you, any day!" Daniel said immediately. His instant loyalty made Noah feel better. "Gabriel's just . . . just . . ." Daniel scowled. "OK, so he's really good at soccer, so what! He made me feel like . . ."

"Incompetent?" Noah suggested quietly. "That's how he always makes me feel."

"What's incompetent mean?" asked Daniel suspiciously.

"Useless," Noah explained. "Like you can't do anything right."

"Yes," Daniel said with a nod. "That's how he made me feel too."

Noah put into words the one thing that neither of them had wanted to mention yet. "And we're playing against him tomorrow. That friendly match . . ."

"Friendly?" Daniel's voice expressed all the doubt Noah was feeling. They weren't feeling very friendly at all.

The next day, it was clear their team knew all about how good Gabriel's team was. They were in the running to win the whole championship, and it seemed ridiculous that they would be playing the worst team in the whole league.

"I've heard we're not even playing their starting lineup," said a teammate as they pulled on their uniforms. "Their coach is putting in a whole team made up of reserves. That's how confident he is."

It was the first time that Daniel and Noah were wearing their team uniforms, but they tried to ignore the twinges of excitement they felt. They were both convinced the game was going to go badly, starting lineup or not.

"No, he's not doing that," corrected Benji, his normally smiling face grim. "My mom heard their coach saying he wants his starters to have, quote, 'an easy win,' unquote."

The player who had originally spoken looked at Benji. "An easy *win*?" he asked. "Not even 'an easy game.' He said win?"

"Win." Benji stood and stamped his feet to settle his soccer shoes. "See you out there."

And, unfortunately, the coach of the opposing team was right in his belief. The entire team played as hard as they could, showing "plenty of passion, but not quite as much skill as could be desired," as Ms. Voss told them with a sigh at halftime. The score was six-zero, Gabriel's team. By the end of the game, the defeat had lengthened to ten-nil, and even the proudest parents on the opposing side had stopped yelling quite so loudly for their kids' goals in the face of Noah's team's utter defeat.

The locker rooms were quiet after the match, and Noah and Daniel both lingered as long as they could with their showering and dressing, hoping the stadium would be deserted when they showed their faces. There were still a few people milling about, but no one that Noah knew. *Dad's probably taken Gabriel somewhere to celebrate his big win,* he thought bitterly. Not wanting to go home, they headed for Grandpa Hugo's. Noah wanted to avoid Gabriel and his dad; Daniel felt unable to fake his usual cheerfulness with his parents, who he was still desperate to reassure about the team being a success.

Grandpa Hugo was sitting on his small porch, watching the birds squawk and squabble over scraps he'd put out for them, but he saw the boys' saddened faces and immediately welcomed them inside.

"What's up?" he asked when he had them sitting in their familiar places at his kitchen table, cookies and glasses of milk in front of them.

"It's Gabriel," Noah said with a heavy sigh, and it was as if those words had been holding back a dam of bitterness and hurt and anger. Now, that dam had broken. Noah talked nonstop for half an hour, explaining how much he resented Gabriel sweeping into his home and monopolizing his dad; always being the best at everything he tried; always being taller, stronger, better looking; and how even Noah's interest in soccer was being tainted by Gabriel's successes on the field. Daniel listened and nodded supportively at the appropriate moments.

"How can I ever hope to compare to Gabriel?" Noah finished, out of breath and out of confidence. "He's so lucky. He gets everything he wants without having to try like I do!" Noah touched his cochlear implant, not saying that he was sure his disability was something else that tainted him: Gabriel's hearing was perfect.

Grandpa Hugo listened quietly to Noah's words. Then, when Noah had finished, he thought before saying, "I'm so sorry you feel this way, Noah. I know your dad doesn't guess any of this. I didn't raise him to play favorites with his children, and he would be horrified to know how upset you are about all of it." He looked at Noah to make sure he had heard and understood his words. Noah nodded reluctantly, suddenly understanding that Grandpa Hugo was his dad's father. He had known it as a fact, but now he understood it in a new and deeper way. But then Grandpa Hugo went on. "However, I would like you *both* . . . ," he shot a sharp glance at Daniel, having picked up on his antagonism toward Gabriel, ". . . to consider, just for a moment, what Gabriel's life is like."

He fell silent for a moment, then continued. "Gabriel was just a little guy when your dad and his mom split up. It was a hard divorce, and she wouldn't let your dad see Gabriel for quite some time. He found that very upsetting and thought your dad was forgetting about him."

#77

"Oh." Noah felt a twinge of sympathy for that little boy, but Grandpa Hugo was still talking.

"Finally, we all came to an agreement that let Gabriel see this side of his family—that is me, your dad, and you. You were just a baby then, so you won't remember any of this."

Noah shook his head. Gabriel had always been around, elegant and handsome, taking up all Dad's time on the weekends when he came to stay.

"But apart from that, Gabriel works really hard to get all those things you were talking about. He studies every night and trains every single day for soccer. He didn't just pick up a soccer ball and have it do tricks for him. That all took hours and hours of work."

Daniel and Noah exchanged uneasy glances. They had been assuming Gabriel was just naturally lucky and talented, but the more they learned about his life, the less lucky Gabriel sounded. Noah wondered what it would be like if his parents split up and he couldn't see one of them, except on special occasions. *It would suck,* he thought.

Daniel had been doing his own thinking. "Our soccer skills have gotten better since we started putting in the work."

"And our schoolwork too," added Noah. "I'm better in some of my subjects than I was before Rosie started helping us with our schedules. I guess Gabriel must do something similar."

"Exactly," said Grandpa Hugo. "It takes a lot of hard work for a long time to get as effortlessly good at anything as Gabriel seems to be. Now. Those cookies didn't fill you up, I guess, and you've both had a hard soccer match. How about some grilled cheese sandwiches for lunch?"

Noah and Daniel agreed that grilled cheese sandwiches would be good, and Grandpa Hugo rummaged around in his large fridge for the cheese.

Daniel said in a low voice, "I guess I wasn't nice to your half-brother."

"My *brother*," corrected Noah. "I wasn't either. I only thought about it from my side. I didn't think about what it must be like for him."

"Yeah." Daniel stared off into space as he thought about something. "I guess our whole team is a bit like that. Too busy looking at how good the other teams are instead of working out how we can be that good."

"Yes," agreed Noah. "Each of us wants to be the best player and score the goals. Did you notice that Gabriel's team doesn't seem to care who scores the goals? They all work together to make sure the ball is in the right place, and then whoever's closest shoots."

"They're better trained than we are," admitted Daniel. "And they know better how to be a team too."

chapter 6

Practice Makes Perfect!

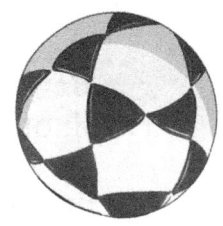

GRANDPA HUGO'S talk, along with Rosie's schedules, had the effect of making sure Noah and Daniel worked harder than ever. The team began to understand their own strengths and weaknesses, and players were assigned to positions that suited them best, rather than being placed somewhere they could do little damage. Noah and Daniel were delighted when their principal made a point of congratulating them for the dramatic improvement in their schoolwork, telling them to keep it up and they would be back up to where they had been in no time.

But perhaps the biggest breakthrough came on the soccer field. Rosie waved to Ms. Voss, asking for a time-out. Ms. Voss blew her whistle and called everyone to her.

When they gathered, looking curiously at Ms. Voss, she shrugged and pointed to Rosie.

Rosie said, "I think we should come up with a system of hand and arm signals we can use on the field."

"OK, but why?" asked one of the players who made a habit of questioning everything.

"Because," said Rosie flatly, "Noah is one of our best players, but he sometimes doesn't hear calls and misses plays because of it. If we use hand and arm signals, not only will that help Noah, but our opponents won't be able to tell what we're saying, so that'll be like a double advantage."

"Oh," the player replied, looking embarrassed and flicking a quick glance at Noah, who had automatically raised a hand to his implant.

It was true: Noah had noticed he sometimes missed calls if he was a distance away from the caller. That often resulted in missing a lead pass or not making himself open to receive the ball. He hadn't been aware that anyone else had noticed, but it figured it was Rosie who'd spotted it. She was hyper aware of everything going on during practices and matches.

Ms. Voss hurried forward, and Noah knew she was embarrassed by Rosie's mention of his disability, so he spoke up quickly.

"That's a good idea, if everyone else agrees," he said. "Yes, it will help me, but hiding our plays from the other team can only be a good thing too, right?"

The rest of the team nodded, relieved Noah wasn't upset, and Rosie beamed happily. She produced a folded-up piece of paper from her pocket.

"Great!" she said. "I've already got the basic moves figured out. We'll work out the rest and then print off enough for everyone to have a copy, OK?"

Rosie worked with Benji and Noah, and soon the whole team had mastered the system of hand signals, even the players who needed to have all the plays explained before they understood their part in them.

As the days flicked past, they began to get nervous about the upcoming championship. It was racing toward them, it seemed, and none of them felt ready.

The championship was a series of matches between all the teams in the region, designed to ensure that every team got to play every other team at least once. It was this championship that the team had come last in every year for the last few years—and the very same championship that Gabriel's team was in the running to win, or at least finish in the top three.

"So, we'll be playing Gabriel's team again?" Daniel asked in dismay.

"Yes, at least once," said Noah. "But honestly, I just want to not come in last."

"How does it work again?" asked one of the players, who generally just enjoyed the time on the field with his friends and didn't care much about the game itself.

"All the teams play two or three games, and then we'll be ranked," Benji explained, as he had been through it all before. "They try to make it so the early games are evenly matched, and then the later ones not so much. Then they'll weed us out to the final sixteen. Then it'll be the quarterfinals, semifinals, and finals."

"Imagine we make it to the finals," a voice from the group of players said wistfully.

"We won't," Rosie answered briskly. "But I'll be happy if we get into the final sixteen."

But even Rosie's modest dream seemed so far out of reach. The team, nervous and stressed, allowed their frustrations to take over. Angry outbursts boiled over on the field, accusations of poor play, missed passes, and bad tackles were thrown around, leading to a huge number of fights. All of Ms. Voss's pep talks and encouragement had no effect, and team morale was at an all-time low by the time the first match rolled around.

As might have been expected, they played terribly. Afterward, all the anger and frustration from the field continued. When Noah found himself the target of both Daniel's and Rosie's yelling, he muted his cochlear implant, leaving himself in blissful silence. They quickly realized he couldn't hear them and instead yelled at each other. If the team had time to unwind before their next match, maybe even had the opportunity to make up and apologize, things might have worked out better. But their next game was in just a few days, and it seemed as though they would have a team where none of the players were actually talking to each other at all.

But Ms. Voss knew she couldn't let that happen. She asked the team to arrive early for the game and gathered them together in a quiet space beyond the soccer field.

"I want you all to remember why you started playing soccer," she started. "Not just on this team, but the first time you ever kicked a ball. None of you were thinking about winning games, or being champions, or even being part of a team. You each first kicked a soccer ball because you loved the game. I want you to dig deep into yourselves and find that part of you again today. I hate the way you've been behaving this last week or so. I would much prefer to lose with grace and good humor and to be good sports rather than win the whole championship if it meant that the spite and nastiness I've seen in the locker room this week is how it's going to be. OK?"

She received a few half-hearted mumbles, but she could see by the red faces and downward glances that her words had struck home. She'd never been truly angry with them, but right now, they realized she was *really* upset. Angry, disappointed, and unhappy because they had all been behaving terribly. They were all sorry for it: they liked Ms. Voss, who was never mean or harsh, and always did *her* best to help them do *their* best. For maybe the first time, they realized Ms. Voss felt just as strongly about their team, the poor reputation they had, and their awful sportsmanship. She was just a lot better at not showing it.

"Soccer is a team sport," she went on more gently. "And until you can work as a team, supporting one another, we'll never get anywhere."

Noah felt sad but was determined to play as best he could to make Ms. Voss proud.

Daniel came up with a different plan. He'd heard about using psychology to make players lose their confidence, and he decided to try it on Gabriel. Therefore, every time he was close to Gabriel, he gave the older boy sneering looks, and snorted rudely when Gabriel kicked the ball. But Gabriel didn't seem to hear or see him—or if he did, he simply didn't care. Daniel thought he saw Gabriel's ears reddening slightly, but he couldn't be sure that wasn't because of the exertions of the game. Frustrated, Daniel decided to step up his campaign.

"Pathetic," he murmured as Gabriel sliced a perfect kick that carried the ball over the halfway line.

"Loser!" he hissed as he ran up behind Gabriel, who was moving into position to intercept a pass. Nothing seemed to work. Gabriel played on as though he wasn't even aware of Daniel's very existence, passing perfectly, intercepting the ball without a flicker of doubt.

"Cheater!" Daniel forgot to whisper and was horrified to hear the referee's whistle sound right behind him. He whirled around and saw the referee raising a yellow card high in the air. Ms. Voss called for a time-out and yelled for the team to huddle up.

"What was that?" She looked at Daniel. "Why did you get a yellow card?"

Daniel blushed bright red, shame suddenly striking him as he realized what he thought was a clever plan was actually mean—and hadn't even worked. "I tried to psych out Gabriel," he mumbled. "I read about it somewhere."

"You don't get carded for psyching someone out," said Ms. Voss. "What did you say?"

Daniel hung his head. "I called him a cheater," he said in a voice so quiet that only Ms. Voss and Rosie could hear him.

She stared at him, her eyes bright with disbelief. "Substitution, please, ref. But I've got no one else to put in, so we'll play a man short for a bit," she called. "Daniel, you're going to come and sit next to me and explain yourself. And if you don't, you won't be playing on my team again."

Daniel nodded, his face the picture of misery, but his humiliation wasn't yet complete.

"You thought it would be cool to call someone names?" Rosie was angry. "You've seen how some of the jerks on the other teams behave when they see they're playing against a girl, and you thought you would do it to someone else?"

Daniel opened his mouth to protest, realized he was completely and utterly in the wrong, and closed it again. He followed Ms. Voss to the sidelines, his shoulders slumped and head hung.

Rosie watched him go, her mouth a thin line of annoyance. Noah tried to comfort her.

"It's not Daniel's fault," he said. "Gabriel has this . . . air . . . about him."

Rosie looked at Noah. "There's no excuse for being a bully."

A few moments later, Gabriel, who was fully aware of what was happening, laughed right into Rosie's face as he raced up to tackle her. Screaming with rage, Rosie lashed out and kicked at Gabriel's leg, forgetting about the ball. Gabriel dodged back, unhurt. But again, the referee had seen the play.

He blew his whistle, showed Rosie a red card, and pointed her off the field.

"What?!" yelled Rosie. "No way! Are you blind? He provoked me!"

The referee glared at her and took his whistle out of his mouth for long enough to say, "Get off my field, young lady, and learn some manners before you return, or you'll never play in this league again."

Rosie stormed off, while the referee called Ms. Voss onto the field. "Get your team to control their emotions and their behavior," he said. "Because at the moment, it's completely unacceptable."

Ms. Voss nodded and returned to the bench. With two of their five strongest players in disgrace, Ms. Voss swerved at the last minute to walk up the field toward the corner. Sitting miserably on the bench, Daniel and Rosie watched her go, glanced at the players on the field, and then looked at their feet. They were ashamed of themselves. Noah, thinking fast, called the players into a quick huddle.

"We have to play as a team, guys," he whispered urgently, keeping one eye on the referee who was retying his shoelaces. "Remember what Ms. Voss said. We have to do our best."

"But those two didn't think of the team, did they?" muttered one of the other players. "And now they're just distracting us!"

Rosie and Daniel were trying to apologize for being carded, but their teammates weren't interested.

Even Noah was feeling abandoned and ignored their hissed sorries. Ms. Voss was still up by the far corner, venting her frustration on a patch of weeds.

In fact, Ms. Voss was much angrier than even Noah could have imagined. But *with herself*, rather than with the team. She had made herself walk away from Daniel and Rosie because she'd known if she had spoken, she would have been utterly furious with them.

"They're not responsible for making your childhood dreams come true, especially poor Rosie," she told herself. "They're just children and they need calm encouragement. Get a grip on yourself!"

Subdued by these events, and the loss of two players, the team actually began to work together. But even with teamwork, there was no miraculous improvement to their game. Noah did his best though, calling out praise and setting up plays, and counted it good luck that the other team only scored twice. Daniel was subbed back on after a few minutes, leaving Rosie drooping sadly at Ms. Voss's side. However, even though they had finally learned to rely on the others and pass the ball to a teammate, they were still outclassed. The score remained 2-0 at the end of the match.

After the game, the team was aware that Ms. Voss was not happy, and they wondered about Rosie and Daniel letting their tempers get the better of them.

But Ms. Voss took a deep breath, smiled at them all, and said, "That was both hideously horrible and much better playing than we've managed so far."

There was a murmur of half-laughs as the tension finally broke.

"And," continued Ms. Voss, "if we can do none of the horrible stuff and more of the better playing, you might actually manage to score a goal in your next match. And wouldn't that be nice?"

chapter 7

Things Fall Apart

DESPITE MS. VOSS ending the game on a positive note, when Noah finished showering, he wanted to find Daniel to discuss how he'd behaved. But there was no sign of him, so he assumed his friend had run off quickly because he didn't want to talk about it. In fact, Daniel was horribly, bitterly ashamed of himself. He had tried to psych out Gabriel, but he had *enjoyed* being mean to the older, better looking, more gifted player. And he *really* didn't like that part of himself.

He saw Rosie, Benji, and Oliver heading for the exit, but even they didn't seem as close as usual. It was more like they were walking together because they were going in the same direction rather than because they were hanging out.

The next day, Benji approached Noah, a worried frown creasing his face. "We need to fix things," he said.

"The team will fall apart if we're always fighting. Rosie's really worried. She feels responsible."

"Daniel won't speak to me," Noah said unhappily. "As soon as he sees me, he races off. Rosie shouldn't have fouled Gabriel, but it wasn't her fault, not really."

They both agreed something must be done, but they didn't know what or how to start the healing process. Noah did what he always did when he had a problem: he went to Grandpa Hugo and spilled the whole sorry story. And as always, Grandpa Hugo listened carefully, asking a few questions to make sure he understood completely, and gave Noah a consoling hug afterward.

"Things like this happen on any team," he said. "You'll find a way through it, especially if you want the team to succeed."

"I do," Noah replied. "But I'm tired of trying to find Daniel. He'll have to come to me."

After Noah had gone home, Grandpa Hugo sat and thought for a long while. He made a phone call, then put on his hat and coat. He was headed to the nearby food court. While he waited for Ms. Voss, he phoned Gabriel. By the end of the day, he had a far more complete picture of the events of the day than Noah had, and he decided it was up to him to fix the friendship between Noah and Daniel. If they could work on themselves to restore their bond, they could work together to fix the team.

"Ah, Noah!" Grandpa Hugo said on Saturday. "I'd like your help today. I want to pull down the old shed to make way for a much bigger greenhouse. I'll get you started tearing down the old one, then just go out and get the last few pieces for the new one. Sound good?"

It seemed odd for Grandpa Hugo to leave Noah to do chores alone, but Noah shrugged and nodded.

A few minutes later, Grandpa Hugo opened the door to Daniel. "Ah, Daniel," he said with a secret smile. "If you would be so kind, I'd like some help tearing down the old shed. Here are some tools. I'll get you started, then go out for some extra supplies, OK?"

"Sure," Daniel said. He was accustomed to being left to work on things alone.

"Great. If you get stuck, there's another helper some-where around here," Grandpa Hugo added. "You'll make quick work of the demolition if you work together."

Daniel nodded, already eyeing the old shed, planning how to make his first move. "Sure, no problem," he said.

Grandpa Hugo rushed around to the other side of the shed where he'd set up Noah with his own tools.

"I've asked someone else to come help," he said casually. "He's on the other side. If you need something, just ask him."

"OK, Grandpa," Noah said, now very confused, but distracted. He was struggling to pull off a plank that seemed to have five hundred nails holding it in place, and he didn't give Grandpa Hugo's strange behavior much thought.

Five minutes later, Grandpa slid into a booth in the ice cream parlor. "Well," he said with a grin. "They're in place. Let's hope it works!"

He beamed around at the others. Rosie, Benji, and Ms. Voss all grinned back. Rosie and Benji showed him their crossed fingers.

Noah and Daniel soon uncovered Grandpa Hugo's plan, when Daniel called for help lifting off a roof truss from one end of the shed. At first, Noah was irritated to see him, but when he realized Daniel had been avoiding him because he was embarrassed, his annoyance quickly faded.

For his part, Daniel understood that a lot of his low feelings were because he had been missing his best friend. Soon, they were rambling away, discussing everything that had happened and how they could move away from this mess. Noah's last remaining doubts were dispelled when he saw that Daniel had learned to face him directly when he spoke, making it easy for Noah to lip-read along with his cochlear-boosted hearing. He paused in what he was saying, suddenly so moved that he could hardly talk, feeling as though he might cry.

Daniel read some of this in his face. "What? What's wrong?"

"I just realized," Noah admitted, "that you've been turning to face me to talk, even though you're still mad at me."

"Mad at you?" Daniel gasped. "No, I'm mad at *me*! What I did to your brother was a jerk move. And I caused Rosie's red card!" He paused, going pink. "But yeah . . . I saw Oliver doing it and . . ." He shrugged. "It makes sense, you know?"

Noah nodded, not saying any more about it. But he found that his hurt and irritation with Daniel had evaporated. Daniel, realizing that Noah hadn't been angry or upset with his foolish actions on the soccer field, was suddenly in a fantastically good mood. They returned to the task Grandpa Hugo had assigned to them with good humor and soon had the old shed stripped down to boards, bricks, and an old paint can filled with bent and broken nails.

While they worked, they resolved all their little grumbles, pointing out areas where the other had shown maturity and growth, and expressed their own feelings of regret, guilt, and disappointment. Finally, they talked about what they had both been like before they met. They agreed that no matter what else had happened, they were both much more grown-up now. All fights forgiven, they made a pact to always look for the positives in situations and to help each other—and the rest of the team—to do the same. Grandpa Hugo arrived shortly thereafter, and the three of them set to work putting up the new greenhouse.

Noah offered to walk with Daniel to his house when they were done so they could continue catching up on all they'd miss during their fight. Daniel said, almost shyly, "You know, we're not done yet, team wise. We can hit one target at least."

"Which one is that?" Noah asked.

"Not finishing dead last," Daniel replied. "If we work

together, the whole team, we can do it." He frowned. "But first I have to apologize to Ms. Voss. I acted terribly."

"I'll apologize too," said Noah. "I only realized how much I'd been trying to be the star player when you and Rosie were off field, and we *had* to pull together."

In agreement, Noah and Daniel made sure they were early for their next practice and apologized to Ms. Voss. She accepted their apologies with warmth and grace. Their teammates, too, accepted their apologies, but left it up to Oliver and Benji to say what they were all thinking. That this year was going to be like every other year. They would most likely finish last. Hearing their comments, Noah and Daniel came up with a plan. With Ms. Voss's OK, they called a nearby school.

At their next practice, the team was amazed to see another soccer team waiting for them.

"Hey, guys," said Daniel. "This is the social soccer team from one of my old schools. They've come by for a friendly game, just for fun. There's no glory here, win or lose, we're just doing it for fun, OK?"

They looked at each other, then shrugged and nodded. Noah knew from their attempt to behave casually that they were actually happy to have a game to play, even though they were pretending to be reluctant.

"Remember," Noah said as Ms. Voss and the other team's coach agreed to co-referee the match, "we're all better players than we were, and having a positive attitude can lead to great achievements!"

The game went well. The team played seamlessly and helped each other out. The set plays worked perfectly. To their immense surprise, Noah and Daniel found themselves leading the cheers when they won the game.

They were careful to be aware of the feelings of the other team—losing always stings—but the other team was happy too.

"We thought soccer was a serious game," the captain said. "But you guys have so much fun on the field. We're going to try and be more like you!"

The captain looked on in puzzlement as Daniel and Noah doubled over with laughter, not understanding their amusement at all.

chapter #8

Making It All Better

THE TEAM'S SPIRIT was fully restored and stronger than ever. Ms. Voss was happy with their sudden progress, especially after the fighting that had been happening.

"Noah, Daniel," she called after practice one day. "I need to pick a captain for the next match. And I think I'll make that person a permanent captain until the end of the championship. Only thing is, I can't choose between you two, and I don't want you fighting over it. What do you think?"

Noah and Daniel exchanged surprised glances, then spoke at the same time. "Rosie!"

"Rosie?" asked Ms. Voss, a little shocked.

"Yes," said Noah. "She helped us with our classwork."

"And I would have dropped out long ago without Rosie's training," added Daniel.

"You think it will be OK, having the one girl on the team as the captain?" Ms. Voss looked undecided.

"I think it will be fine having our *best player* as captain," said Daniel. "And in our case, that's Rosie!"

Noah nodded, and Ms. Voss smiled. "Great, Rosie it is, then," she said. "And you're both co-vice-captains, OK?"

Rosie could be tough on her team, but Ms. Voss's trust in making her captain seemed to settle her. She turned out to be great, quickly moving players to boost their strengths and hide any weaknesses.

It was with high hopes that the team ran out onto the field for their next match in the championship. Ms. Voss and Rosie warned everyone.

"They're a really strong team," said Ms. Voss.

"Yeah," added Rosie. "They're in the running to win the whole championship. So, we're unlikely to win this one."

"But just do your best," Ms. Voss continued. "And have fun!"

The team played well, but the other team was indeed stronger and beat them—but only by one goal.

Ms. Voss was delighted to overhear the opposing coach fretting that his team hadn't won by a wider margin, saying that they must not be as strong as he'd thought. She took great joy in telling him, "Or maybe, my team is much better than they were last year, and your team is just fine." Then she walked back to her team, a proud grin lighting up her face.

"Mom!" Benji exclaimed teasingly, in mock-amazement. "Are you sashaying? My mother, sassy and sashaying down the field?"

"Oh, hush!" Ms. Voss laughed, but the proud smile stayed on her face for the rest of the day.

The high from the narrow loss carried them into the weekend and to Daniel's birthday party. His parents, somewhat bemused by Daniel's urgent insistence, agreed he could have friends over to enjoy his birthday, and his dad ordered party supplies and a big colorful cake. For once, he actually had a big gang of friends (including, of course, the entire team) that he knew well enough to invite to his party, so he could have a proper celebration.

While waiting for everyone to show up, Daniel panicked a little when he misread his watch and thought no one was coming. But his mom soon pointed out that it was only ten past eleven, and the invites had said twelve.

After that, he relaxed a lot, but was still nervous until there was a tap at the door and Noah, Rosie, Benji, and Oliver all walked in. They were stiff and awkward in their nicest clothes, all carrying beautifully wrapped presents for Daniel. The birthday boy stared at the shiny presents with an overwhelmed expression.

"Guys!" he said. "Thanks for coming! Presents too? Aw . . . man!" He choked up a little and found he didn't care. He didn't mind if his friends saw he was feeling emotional: he trusted them completely.

Unseen by Daniel, however, were his parents, who were peeking out in fascination at the children. They had become so accustomed to Daniel's solitary existence that the discovery he not only had friends, but close friends, had come as a huge surprise to them.

"He's so happy!" Dad said fondly.

"Yes," Mom agreed. "I wonder if we've maybe moved around too much."

"Maybe. But we need to move for our work, dear."

"I suppose we do." Mom frowned. "But I think Daniel needs to settle down sometime soon. If not here, then in a year or two at the latest. We'll have to make arrangements with our jobs. *Oh!* I'd better go put the candles

on the cake and bring it in! I almost forgot the whole mom-in-charge-of-birthdays thing!"

A moment later, Daniel's face glowed almost enough to outshine the candles as Mom carefully carried the cake to where he was sitting at the head of the table. Dad started a high-energy rendition of "Happy Birthday," which all Daniel's friends joined.

"Go on." Mom smiled. "Make a wish!"

"Right!" Daniel grinned. He thought for a second. He closed his eyes, leaned forward, and muttered, almost under his breath, "I wish we make it to the semifinals and that we can stay here forever!" Then he blew out all the candles with one mighty puff, earning himself cheers and catcalls from his teammates.

Mom looked at Dad, raising her eyebrows significantly. Dad nodded, understanding that look to mean, "We have to talk."

chapter #9

A Testing Time

CHEERED BY THE SUCCESS of Daniel's party and the team finally understanding what teamwork actually meant, the next few practice sessions went well. Even Ms. Voss was hard-pressed to take the big, beaming smile off her face.

"It's going great," Noah said with a laugh to Daniel as they came out of the locker rooms after practice. "I'm beginning to think something's going to go wrong, just to keep us in our places."

"Yeah!" Daniel laughed too and drew breath to continue, but he was interrupted by Rosie's voice from behind them.

"Hey, you two!"

They turned to see what she wanted.

"Here." She thrust weekly sheets at them.

"Oh, the old one's still good..." Noah began, then his voice trailed off as he took in the title Rosie had added to this one. Daniel had spotted it too.

"Tests?" he yelped. "Review? Test review timetable? Rosie, this is impossible!" He jabbed a finger at his sheet. "You've given us even more schoolwork!"

"Yep." Rosie looked at him calmly. "Want to pass?"

"I do," Noah said, still looking at his schedule. "Thanks, Rosie." But his cheerful mood had evaporated, and he felt a familiar nervous squirm in his stomach. Even though he had been working hard and using Rosie's strict schedule, he was still falling behind in geography. A solid string of Cs had risen only to C-plus, even with all the extra work he was putting in. Ideally, he needed to get it up to a solid B—he could squeak by with a B-minus—to meet his parents' expectations of an A average overall. He looked at Rosie and Daniel. "I still need to do a lot better in geography. It's my weakest subject, and it's pulling down my overall grade."

Without hesitating, Daniel said, "It's my best subject! The only thing I'm getting an A in. I'll help you, Noah. We can study together." He and Noah scanned their new schedules again. They noticed there was even less spare time and so much more studying, but, thankfully, still a decent amount of soccer time.

"There," said Daniel, pointing to a two-hour chunk on a Wednesday afternoon. "We can study together on Wednesdays, and we can review geography then."

Noah nodded happily, wordlessly bumping his shoulder against Daniel's to express his gratitude. Daniel slung an arm around Noah's neck and playfully mock-punched his shoulder.

"Ugh, boys," deadpanned Rosie, rolling her eyes, but with an affectionate gleam.

"Thanks, Rosie," Noah said again. "This will be a huge help."

The next few weeks passed in a blur of reviewing, note-taking, flashcard making, and reading, along with precious hours of soccer where the team trained and played better than ever before. When he had the opportunity to think about it, Noah realized he was having a wonderful time, despite the low-level nerves and constant tiredness.

Finally, it was time for their last test. It felt strange to see all the desks arranged in lines, instead of the cheerful groups they were used to. It was even stranger to hear how silent it could be: just the footsteps of the teacher and the sleepy buzzing of a bee that had found itself trapped in the classroom.

At last, "Pencils down, pass your papers forward," sounded, and the teacher said they were free to go. The classroom swiftly emptied.

Daniel looked at Noah and stretched his arms over his head, a broad grin splitting his face. "Well, come on. Let's get out of here and relax for once."

Noah smiled back at him. "Yes! Just hang on a sec, though." Noah opened one of the windows, and using a spare piece of paper, carefully ushered the bee toward the opening. It buzzed frantically against the page, panicking for a moment, then spotted the open window and escaped. Noah watched it go, then closed the window again, turning back to Daniel.

"My place?" he asked. "Well, Grandpa Hugo's, at least?"

"Excellent idea," Daniel said.

Now that they were done studying for their tests, time seemed to slow down, painfully. A week crawled past, but at last, the teachers announced that test results would be handed out after lunch, after the office staff

added them to the students' records. Noah's stomach immediately started squirming. He saw that even Daniel, who normally offered a very believable "don't-care" attitude when it came to his schoolwork, looked more than a little bit nervous.

"Why couldn't they hand them out *before* lunch?" grumbled Daniel, eyeing his bologna sandwich with a queasy expression. "I'm too nervous to eat, but I'll be starving in class if I don't."

"I'll be sick if I eat and then don't pass," muttered Noah. "You'll be fine, though. Your parents are already happy with the work you've done."

"Yeah," Daniel said with a nod. "But the test results will be proof that what I've been telling them is the truth. What if I failed everything? They'll think I was lying and keep me from playing soccer ever again."

They were relieved when the bell rang. All the students rushed to look at the test results that had been placed on their homeroom desks. Holding his breath, Noah snatched his up and ran his finger down to geography, ignoring all the other subjects for now. *B-plus!* His breath whooshed out in a relieved gust, and he looked at Daniel whose face had gone pink. He was smiling, so Noah took that to mean a good thing.

"Safe?" Daniel asked, raising an eyebrow.

Noah nodded, now letting himself look at the rest of his grades. He was happy to see mainly As, with geography and art his only B-pluses, which he knew his parents wouldn't mind. "Did OK," he said. "Thank goodness!"

"Me too," said Daniel. "Two As, two Cs, everything else Bs. My parents will be happy with that."

"Awesome!" They high fived each other and then hurried to get to their next class, Daniel stuffing an entire sandwich in his mouth as he went.

After school, they gathered Rosie, Oliver, and Benji—all of whom had done well—and went to celebrate their improved results with pizza and ice cream. As always, it wasn't long before Oliver mentioned the next stage of the championship. Thanks to their improved playing, they had met Rosie's dream of making it into the final sixteen for the first time ever. The waitress, who kindly brought them endless refills on their drinks without being asked, overheard Benji talking about their next match.

"Oh," she said. "Which team do you play for?"

When they told her, she made a face at first, but then reconsidered. "Actually," she said, "I've heard you're a lot better than last year's team."

"That's not hard," said Benji with a laugh. "We are a *lot* better. We've got some decent players and a great captain." Rosie blushed a delicate shade of pink "And even the, uh, less-skilled guys understand how to work as a team now." He looked around the table proudly.

"Cool," the waitress replied. "If you make it to the quarterfinals, I'll cheer for you." Then she loaded her tray with empty glasses and plates and vanished into the kitchen.

Oliver and Daniel blinked, bemused by her attitude, but Rosie and Benji giggled.

"The people here don't really care about the championship until the quarterfinals," explained Rosie. "By then, they're likely to see some really good games." She paused for a moment, then said in a quieter voice, "I've always watched the last stages from the stands."

There was a respectful silence in which they all thought that maybe this time they would take part in some of those "really good games."

Later that week, Ms. Voss piled the team into the school's minibus. They drove one town over where the championship draw was being held for the next stages. They clustered together, seeing with amazement that even the polished players of the top five teams looked just as nervous as they felt. Noah noticed Gabriel with his team and nodded a stiff acknowledgment. Gabriel, with his jaw clenched, raised a hand back to him.

Rosie whispered, "A bad draw here can mean they end up fighting for third and fourth instead of in the final."

Gabriel's team was called, and they immediately huddled around each other, listening intently. Their opponents would be . . .

Ms. Voss's team!

There was an audible groan from the team, hearing they would be facing their old nemesis so soon in the competition. But Ms. Voss plastered a bright smile on her face and whispered to them to smile and go shake hands with the other team.

"Good sportsmanship is just as important as playing well," she said. "Go and acknowledge them."

It was hard to get their attention, though. Gabriel and his teammates were jumping up and down with joy, loudly cheering and celebrating. Clearly, they thought they were in for another easy win. But they did stop long enough to shake hands, and Noah found himself face-to-face with Gabriel.

"Good luck," Gabriel said, seeming almost surprised to hear the words coming out of his own mouth.

"You too," Noah replied automatically.

But on the bus home, the team swore that even if they did lose to Gabriel's team again, this time would be a much harder fight.

Back at the school, Ms. Voss looked at her watch and said there wasn't really time for any exercises and that everyone could head home early, unless they wanted to kick around the ball for twenty minutes. Daniel and Noah were about to join the trickle of their teammates heading out of the gates when a "Psst!" came from behind them.

"Rosie?" Daniel asked curiously. "Why are you hiding in the bushes?"

"Shh!" Rosie said sharply and grabbed them each by the hand to pull them toward her, out of sight of Ms. Voss who was parking the minibus in its usual spot. "I want to talk to you about something!"

Two days later, the sun rose before Noah did, but barely. His eyes popped open as the first sunbeam lit up his bedroom wall. Instantly wide-awake, he knew that trying to get back to sleep was useless. He got up and texted the group chat, but no one replied.

"Still sleeping," Noah said to himself. "Fair."

Time eventually passed, and as soon as Daniel replied in the group message that he was heading down to the soccer field, Noah set off too. He left a note for his parents who would be coming to watch the match after they woke up and had a leisurely breakfast.

Noah and Daniel were quickly joined by the other team members, and they all clustered together nervously, looking at the huge crowd that accumulated a full hour before kickoff. Noah watched parents shooing their young children along the rows and saw there were vendors selling snacks and mementos like balloons, T-shirts, and more. The PA system squawked to life and pop music played in the background, adding a carnival air to the event.

Time crawled by so slowly that it was almost a relief when the teams were called to line up, ready to run onto the playing field. As Noah and Daniel stood behind Rosie, who was leading them on, Noah saw two players on Gabriel's team yawning widely. In fact, there was something less disciplined about them this time. Noah leaned forward and pointed this out to Rosie, who swept the whole team with a single glance before nodding once.

At last, the game was under way and the referee released the ball. Moving like lightning, not using any of the hand and arm signals they had come up with, Rosie streaked forward, intercepting the ball from one of the players who had been yawning. He stopped, confused and wondering where the ball had gone, but she was already flying down the field, the ball seemingly glued to her toe. While Gabriel's team was in disarray, unsure of what was going on because she had moved so fast, Rosie slowed, took the time to measure her shot, and kicked the ball hard and true into the right-hand top corner of the net.

"Goal!" the referee shouted and blew his whistle.

There was a moment of dead silence, then a storm of applause as the crowd took in and appreciated Rosie's bold goal. Noah, Daniel, and the rest of the team converged on Rosie whose face was a picture of delight.

"I pulled it off!" She grinned. "I wasn't sure if it would work. I wasn't sure if I was fast enough!"

"That was awesome, Rosie!" Benji cried.

The referee indicated that the team should return to their positions, and they did, proud smiles on their faces and the crowd utterly on their side.

But Gabriel's team had learned their lesson. Alarmed at being behind so early in the game, they tightened up their defense so much that Noah and Daniel could hardly move. Within ten minutes of intense play, one of Gabriel's teammates scored an equalizer and the game was even. Play moved up and down the field, both teams fighting hard and refusing to budge an inch. Rosie played tactically, swapping players around to make the most of their strengths and responding to the opposing players' movements, but they never again enjoyed the easy advantage that she had taken her chance on earlier.

By the time the whistle blew for halftime, players on both sides were showing signs of fatigue. Noah noticed that even Gabriel was hot and sweaty, his usually perfectly coiffed hair sticking up and his cheeks streaked with bright red. The team filed into the locker room and slumped on the benches, eating their snack of oranges and sipping water in silence.

The opposing team was also in their locker room, just next door, and they were not silent at all! The team captain could be overheard, berating his team, screaming at them for not being goals ahead by now. His teammates tried to defend themselves, but he yelled over them, insulting them, until his coach came in.

"Stop yelling, Roger! Guys, you're playing as well as ever. Keep it up."

"But we're not ahead!" complained Roger. "Last time we were ahead by six goals against the same team! I've checked, they've got the same players and everything."

The team stirred a little, Daniel's broad grin the biggest and brightest by only a small margin.

"Yes," rumbled the coach in his deep, baritone voice, "the same team. The same team that has been hitting the field three times a week without fail since our last meeting, putting in the time and the practice and getting better and better. I'll tell you guys frankly; I'm seriously impressed with the team you're playing. That opening goal was magic! They've got the motivation, and that's given them the skills to play seriously well. Teams like that are the reason I always tell you never to get complacent."

The coach moved away, and they couldn't catch any more of what he was saying: but they didn't need to. They were delighted with his words. Because he hadn't been speaking to them, they realized that it must be true—he wasn't just being polite. When Ms. Voss finally spoke, they all jumped. They had been concentrating on the drama unfolding next door so much that they hadn't noticed her come in.

"He's right, you know," she said, her own face beaming with pride and happiness. "Even if you lose the second half by a dozen goals, you've already played so much better than ever before. I'm very proud of you all. You should be proud of yourselves too!"

Her words had an even more energizing effect than their snacks, and soon, they were ready to get back on the field to finish the game.

Play resumed as though there had never been a break: Gabriel's team was tightly focused and determined, but so was Noah's. The game rippled and moved from one side to the other. Skirmishes formed around the goals but never amounted to anything before the tide turned and swept the ball and players up the field to the other goal. Noah kept an eye on the massive clock that was counting down the minutes. It was just two minutes until the end of the game. Would the team be playing their first ever overtime period?

One minute.

Suddenly, Gabriel feinted around Rosie, sending the ball one way and himself the other. She hesitated, unsure of whether to mark her man or follow the ball, and that gave Gabriel the millisecond he needed to sweep in and retrieve it. He picked it up, sprinting at full speed down the field, in perfect control of the ball while dodging players as he wove in and out the whole way. By the time he got to the edge of the penalty area, the goalie and the backs were waiting for him. Gabriel took a split-second to calculate his options, and then confidently kicked the ball. It flew fast and high over the heads of the backs, curving ever so slightly. With his eyes on the ball, the goalie attempted to intercept it. But the ball was a black-and-white blur as it spun toward him, seemingly bending just out of his grasp. It came to land with a *whoosh* in the net, just as the whistle blew for the end of the game.

As one, the crowd leaped to their feet, their united gasp of amazement morphing into a roar of approval and admiration. Noah stared at Gabriel, his mouth open in shock, and found that instead of being upset, he was tremendously proud of his brother. Daniel ran past Noah and grabbed Gabriel's hand.

"That. Was. Amazing!" Daniel yelled. "Better than Messi! Congratulations!"

"Thanks?" Gabriel was jolted by Daniel's enthusiastic handshakes, but he was smiling—exhausted but happy.

Noah ran to join them. "It was," Noah added a little incoherently. "It really was. Best goal!"

"Thanks, Noah," said Gabriel. "You guys were really good too. You've improved so much, it's incredible! And your captain who scored your goal? She's a fantastic player. What's her name? I'd like to say good job to her."

"Rosie," Noah replied. "I think she'd like that."

After they had all shaken hands and congratulated anyone they could see, the team trailed into the locker room to shower and change. They were all still there, combing their hair and finding excuses to stay—no one wanted this moment to stop—when Ms. Voss came in, tears in her eyes.

"Ms. Voss?" Noah asked in alarm. "What's wrong?"

"Because it was such a close game," Ms. Voss started, "we've received two championship points instead of one."

Daniel didn't understand. "What does that mean?"

"It means we're not last!" announced Ms. Voss. "Another team lost by more than five goals in two of their games, so they're officially out of the competition with one point as their final result."

#125

It took a moment for what Ms. Voss was saying to trickle through, but Benji finally grinned widely. "We're not bottom of the list anymore? Hooray!"

"And we've still got more games to play!" Daniel added. "If we can hold our own again . . ."

And they managed to not only hold their own but actually win two of their five games. Daniel scored one of the winning goals while his parents were watching and was so proud of himself that he very nearly burst. Noah, who had generously set up the goal for him, was genuinely happy for his friend. The team—win or lose—played their hardest in every game, and the judging panel took note of it. To their absolute delight, the team was awarded fourth place overall before they settled down together to watch Gabriel's team take on the current champions. A lot of the crowd had seen Gabriel's almost-miraculous goal and was firmly on his team's side—as was Noah! And they screamed and roared along with the crowd when Gabriel's team scored early on and maintained that lead, lengthened it after halftime, and all the way to the final whistle.

chapter #10

A Happy Ending?

FINALLY, THE HUGE, good-tempered crowd thinned out, and soon there were only players and their families left. Gabriel was spending the weekend with his dad, so he waved goodbye to his team and hung back when Ms. Voss came over, trying to round up her team.

"Come on!" she said cheerfully. "We're celebrating! My treat because my team has done so amazingly well this year."

"Oh, my parents are here," Daniel said awkwardly, indicating his parents who were talking animatedly to Noah's parents.

"Parents too!" said Ms. Voss. "And family members." She beamed at Gabriel who smiled back gratefully. She added, "That goal was fantastic, young man. Well done!"

"Thanks," he said with a casual shrug. Noah was amused to see that Gabriel was blushing.

With parents in agreement, they all headed off to the pizza parlor, packing it and spilling out onto the outdoor terrace. Daniel, Noah, and Gabriel ended up at the same side of the table, and this time they included Gabriel in their chat, joking and teasing one another. Gabriel seemed pleased to be included, but Noah noticed him frown in confusion from time to time.

Finally, he asked, "Gabriel, what's up? You seem . . . worried."

"Oh." Gabriel blushed a little again. "No, it's just . . . I thought you hated soccer. And I didn't know you could be fun like this." He blushed more deeply. "I'm sorry, that sounds mean. I didn't mean it like that. Just that . . . you always leave the room when I'm there, and you don't really watch the games with us."

"I *want* to!" Noah exclaimed without thinking about it. "But it's always been like . . . *your* thing with Dad. I didn't want to intrude if you didn't want me there."

"Wow." Gabriel blinked several times. "I . . . I guess we just thought you didn't like soccer. I thought you were only playing to make Dad happy."

"Mmm." Noah hummed, thinking about it. "It started like that, I think. But I found that I really like it."

"You're good too," Gabriel offered generously and sincerely. "We should play together." He glanced at their dad who was watching them with a hopeful expression on his face. "And definitely come and watch the games on TV with us. Dad always hogs the popcorn, but between us, we can make sure we get our fair share."

"He does, doesn't he?" said Noah, feeling a surge of affection for Gabriel. For the first time, he really understood they were brothers.

They burst out laughing and looked at their dad who smiled at them happily, obviously overjoyed their long-standing feud was at an end.

Noah munched on a slice of pizza and looked down the table at his teammates and their families. It seemed that every single person was discussing the tournament, shouting out their favorite player, the best goal, and the slickest moves they'd seen. As he chewed on the crust, he heard Ms. Voss call out to Rosie.

"Rosie! I've been meaning to ask. What on earth were you doing the other day? I was parking the minibus and I saw you dragging Noah and Daniel away."

Rosie blushed as everyone turned to stare at her, then she said, "I was waiting until a bit later, but I guess now is as good a time as any."

Noah remembered how Rosie had grabbed his and Daniel's hands and tugged them around the corner, out of sight of the minibus.

"Guys," Rosie had said that day, "I've been thinking. Ms. Voss has been working with this team for three or four years now. Before she was hired by the school, she did it for free, putting in her own money and time, and the team has always been terrible." Rosie had frowned. "She's also been trying really hard to get a girls' team going. A lot of my friends say they'll play if there's a girls' team. Ms. Voss hasn't been able to get any funding or support for it. I know it really upsets her."

"What can we do?" Noah had asked, feeling a stab of sympathy for their coach.

"I want to get her a present to show our appreciation. Something nice," Rosie continued. "But obviously, I can't do it all myself. I can maybe afford a bunch of flowers, but that's it. So, do you guys think the others would want to chip in so we can get her something nice?"

"Yes," Daniel said immediately. "Here, I'll message the group chat."

And, indeed, everyone on the team had agreed that Ms. Voss deserved an amazing present. Pretty soon,

Rosie had an envelope packed with enough money to buy something really good.

Returning to the present, Rosie said, "I wanted to ask the guys about getting you something for being the best coach and mentor any soccer player could ever have. And they all agreed, so we got you this."

Rosie handed Ms. Voss a large gift bag, from which Ms. Voss pulled out a big, beautiful vase in the shape of a woman carrying the world on one shoulder.

"Oh, it's wonderful!" Ms. Voss exclaimed, admiring the delicate design. She stored it back in the bag and looked up, smiling all around at everyone. She took a breath to say something but astonished herself—and everyone else—by bursting into tears. As she mopped her eyes and assured everyone they were happy tears, Daniel's parents came over to Noah to introduce themselves.

"We wanted to thank you for befriending Daniel," said his mom.

"He's a good friend," Noah replied. "He really helped me with my geography." He looked around the table. "And he helped me join the team and make friends."

Daniel, a trace of anxiety on his face at seeing his parents talking to his friend, came over.

"Daniel," his mom said, turning to him. "We've noticed that you seem to like it here."

Daniel began to nod eagerly, but she went on.

"So, we've been thinking. This is actually a pretty good, central place. We could stay here for a few years if you'd like. As long as you don't mind me or Dad going away for a few days at a time, now and then. Separately, of course. We don't think you're quite ready to be home alone yet."

Daniel grinned so widely that Noah wondered if it was possible for a person's face to split in half.

"Yes, I am," Daniel teased his mom. "I'll take care of the house."

"I bet you will," his dad said with a laugh. "Nice try, son. But would you like that? Staying put for a bit?"

For once speechless and overwhelmed, Daniel leaned against his dad, nodding his head vigorously. He reached out and pulled his mom into the hug too.

She moved in willingly, saying to the table, with a laugh, "Well! We've been trying to silence this kid for years! Seems like we've finally found out how to do it."

The wave of laughter swept the whole table, and even Daniel joined in, laughing until tears filled his eyes.

Later, there were some messages in the group chat.

Noah: Rosie, Daniel. Can you meet me?

Rosie: Sure, where?

Noah: School gate?

Daniel: Yeah, see you there.

Rosie: On my way.

At the school, Daniel saw that Rosie and Noah were already there. Rosie had an intrigued expression on her face, and Noah was holding a folder.

"Whatcha got there?" Daniel asked.

"It's a petition," said Noah. "I asked my mom and dad how you make things happen, and they said you make a petition stating what you want. Then you get lots of people to sign it if they agree with you, and you take your petition to, like, the mayor or whoever, and if there are lots of signatures, they'll make it happen."

"Petition for what?" Rosie asked. "What do you want?"

"A girls' soccer league," Noah said simply. "We can start small with just a few girls' teams. I think that would be pretty good. But eventually, maybe a girls' championship."

"I like it!" Rosie exclaimed, her face lighting up. She took the pages from Noah's folder and read through them carefully. "Ms. Voss as president? Yes!" She read on. "Me as her second-in-command? Really?"

Noah nodded.

"This is really cool!" Rosie replied. "But why are you doing it? You're a boy, you've already got a club and a league."

"I was worried," said Noah, "on the first day of school. I was scared I wouldn't make friends. That I'd never be good at any sport. That I'd hate it all . . ." He paused, staring at the empty folder in his hand. "But the club changed that. I made friends with Daniel, and you, and Benji. I met up with Oliver again—and all the other guys. I'm so happy now compared to before. I don't want anyone, boy or girl, to feel left out and lonely like I used to feel."

Rosie and Daniel nodded understandingly and agreed that a girls' soccer league was a fantastic idea.

"We could share the fields," said Rosie, finding a map of the school grounds. "But they'll have to build a girls' locker room. I always have to use the teachers' facilities at soccer games. That sucks! But there's space there, see?"

"Yes," Daniel replied. "We'll need to get some money. Maybe the city council. I know!" He beamed at them. "I'll get my mom to write a piece for the newspaper saying how there's a demand for girls' soccer teams. Maybe that will help raise interest and support."

"Excellent!" said Rosie.

The three of them bent their heads over the petition, and the sun shined behind them, sending long, slanting rays of light over their huddle. It threw them into silhouette and made them seem to be a single, multiheaded creature, united in desire and purpose.

Each book that we have published has
a free audio version available. To download
the audiobook for *The Worst Team Ever*,
all you have to do is scan the QR code
or visit: www.littlebigpage.com/team

If you have any problems
or questions, feel free to contact
us at help@littlebigpage.com

MEET THE BOYS WHO WILL SHOW YOU HOW TO BE YOURSELF EVERY DAY!

ARISE, MY AMAZING BOY

"Young readers are invited to enjoy..."
—Readers' Favorite

MATEO SOMMER

MORE ABOUT THE BOOK

Made in the USA
Las Vegas, NV
25 April 2026

45861016R00079